EXPLORING PAUL'S LETTERS

Galatians to Philemon

Phil Crowter

DISCOVER PUBLICATIONS

DISCOVER PUBLICATIONS

Arisaig, Crowborough Hill, Crowborough, E. Sussex, TN6 2LS, England

© Discover Publications 1995

First published 1995

Scripture quotations:
New King James Bible
© Thomas Nelson Inc. 1984

ISBN: 0 9524448 0 1

CONTENTS

	page
Galatians	7
Ephesians	29
Philippians	54
Colossians	72
1 Thessalonians	89
2 Thessalonians	106
1 Timothy	115
2 Timothy	133
Titus	146
Philemon	154
Map	158

PREFACE

Perhaps I was foolish to attempt it. A tall order, but one that needed to be met. A kind of commentary and daily devotions rolled into one. Something that is serious with the Bible and yet gives some day-to-day practical help. A book that tackles the bits you didn't understand and yet makes you think too. All squashed into a single page for a day-sized reading.

I hope and pray I have at least begun to succeed. Enough for you to start to get a grip on the message of these amazing letters. Enough to excite you to dig deeper into God's Word.

Use this book how you like. It will keep you busy for four months of daily readings, or if you prefer, just dip into it when your own reading programme reaches Ephesians or Titus or ...

I think you might find it valuable too as a starter for group Bible study, or as back-up material for a sermon series.

One last request. For maximum benefit try to find that extra 15 - 30 minutes to read each letter through in one sitting before beginning to study it - and to tackle the outline summary when you have reached the end. The effort will be well rewarded!

Philip Crowter

DISCOVER PUBLICATIONS,
September 1995

If you find this book enriches your Bible reading, you may like to try EXPLORE daily Bible reading notes - see page 160.

FACT - FILE : *Galatians*

> **Galatians**
>
> No additions!

THE CHURCH

- Not a single church, but a group of churches probably in S. Galatia (including Antioch, Iconium, Lystra, Derbe - see map on page 158).
- These were churches founded by Paul on his first missionary journey, around AD 48 (Acts 13, 14). It was particularly the Gentiles who had responded to the gospel.
- They were still young churches, and heavily influenced by teachings from Jerusalem, which tried to add Jewish traditions to the faith of the Gentile Galatian Christians. It was just the issue that Paul sorted out with the other apostles at the Jerusalem conference in Acts 15 - although it is uncertain whether the Galatian letter was written before or after this.

THE LETTER

- Probably written during Paul's second missionary journey, around AD 52.
- Written to combat the error of the Jerusalem teachers, who claimed that the mark of circumcision was necessary to authenticate the faith of the Gentile believers. Paul insists that nothing can be added to 'improve on' faith in Christ alone; adding to the gospel makes it no gospel at all.
- Chapters 1 and 2 **establish Paul's authority** as an apostle, to insist on this truth.

   Chapters 3 and 4 **argue the case**, based on Old Testament scriptures.

   Chapters 5 and 6 **lay out the consequences**; a Spirit-controlled life.
- See fuller outline at the end of the section.

If at all possible ...

Find time to read the letter through in one sitting, with this background in mind.

Meaningful greeting! *Galatians 1 v 1 - 5*

Paul's opening verses are not just a nice way of beginning a letter, with no real point to them. Careful reading shows they are highly charged, as Paul goes straight in with key themes the Galatians believers need to sort out -

Read v 1 - 5.

PAUL, AN APOSTLE ...

Who is this Paul you listen to? What right has he to insist on sole knowledge of the truth? He is wrenching you away from the Jewish roots of your faith! Such were the likely claims of some among the Galatians. They were seeking to undermine Paul's authority, to win people round to accept their more 'authentic' gospel.

Paul sees clearly that not just his reputation but the whole gospel of Jesus Christ is at stake. They must accept his authority as God's apostle; not self-appointed or chosen by other believers, but dramatically called out by the risen Jesus.

We are still under apostolic authority. Not man-appointed modern-day so-called apostles, but the apostles' teaching in the Bible. We are not free to pick and choose the bits we like; Paul and the other apostles spoke with God's own authority. Reject Paul and you reject the gospel of salvation.

GRACE TO YOU, AND PEACE ...

Rich, glorious words - never take them for granted! Never let go of the idea that salvation comes to us totally free and undeserved, out of God's sheer **grace**. Never stop praising God for the **peace** which Christ alone has brought us through His cross.

Favourite words of Paul - and of all true believers. But unpopular with those, like the Galatian false teachers, who wish to mix in something of their own contribution. Unpopular because unknown; God never gives His priceless gifts to those who are not sure they need them ...

WHO GAVE HIMSELF FOR OUR SINS ...

Can you see how Paul is exciting the love and praise of the true believers in the Galatian churches? If only they would get back to what Christ had done for them they would not fall for any 'additional requirements' that would make their faith the 'real thing'. Why, our sins have already been dealt with. Christ has rescued us from this evil age and made us part of His glorious kingdom! He has done it - there is nothing for us to contribute.

Has Christ rescued you? If so you might like to think through what 'evil' He has rescued you from. What responses are called for?
Read Titus 2 v 14, 3 v 3 - 7.

One response is surely inevitable! *To whom be glory forever and ever. Amen!'* (v 5)

No other gospel! *Galatians 1 v 6 - 10*

What is missing from this letter? Look at Paul's other epistles to churches and you will find a burst of thankfulness for the believers. (See Ephesians 1 v 15, 16; Philippians 1 v 3, 4; Colossians 1 v 3, 4 etc). Contrast that with v 6 in Galatians 1 to get a feel for the seriousness of the problems there! This was no minor deviation needing a bit of straightening out - Paul was fighting an issue that threatened to lure whole churches from the gospel itself. Warning not thanksgiving was in order!

Read v 6 - 10.

Another gospel is no gospel at all (v 6, 7).

Pure water is good news indeed at the end of a hot afternoon. A drop of poison might just improve the taste and would certainly quench your thirst just the same, but would turn good news into deadly news. The 'original' gospel is the only gospel (good news). The 'new improved taste' versions can only spell death, for any additions turn the pure gospel into no gospel at all.

Why? Because any additions are our own additions - and therefore can never satisfy a holy God.

Why? Because any additions claim to add to **Christ's** perfect, complete salvation - and adding to perfection always ruins it.

Paul is astonished at the Galatians. How could anyone who has tasted the pure, free 'grace of Christ' desert the Saviour in favour of their own miserable efforts! Be completely clear about this; there **is** no alternative gospel - all other alternatives are deadly, damning news.

Cursed be all who teach it! (v 7 - 9).

This is no outburst of rage, no over-zealous exaggeration. However popular, however renowned, however influential the preacher might be, the curse of an angry God rests on him as soon as he suggests alternatives to salvation by grace. Such people are not merely 'mistaken' or 'mostly right' - they are 'accursed'. A shocking description, but a moment's thought shows why it is the only accurate one. They are cursed because they are leading others to hell. *Read Matthew 7 v 21 - 23; 15 v 7 - 9, 12 - 14; 23 v 13, 15.*

Not an easy way to begin his letter! Not the way to win friends, or to make people feel warm towards him! So why does Paul speak so sharply? *Read v 10 again.*

Paul is not in the business of pleasing men! His enemies might well accuse him of using cunning arguments to persuade others onto his side, but his language is hardly that of someone whose concern is popularity!

As soon as we become men-pleasers, we cease to be servants of Christ ...

Revelation from Jesus *Galatians 1 v 11 - 24*

'It's not my message but God's' should be a dominant theme in any Christian's testimony. Why should others listen to our views rather than everyone else's - unless we appeal to a higher authority? And we need not only to **claim** we are passing on God's message, but to **show** them that we are, from the Bible. Can you do that?

It was crucial for Paul to prove to the Galatians that the gospel he preached was no man-made message, but came with God's own authority. But of course he could not simply point to the Bible for proof, because the New Testament did not exist - Paul was one of the apostles God inspired to write much of it! No, he had to demonstrate that it was Jesus Himself who had personally revealed the gospel to him, and commissioned him to broadcast it as God's own message -

Read v 11 - 24.

Look at my conversion! (v 13 - 16)

Paul was the last person in the world who would have made up the gospel - and the last person the other apostles could have persuaded to join their ranks! Nothing could have been more abhorrent to his bigotted Pharisaical mind than God's free grace. Nothing could have been so inconceivable as to devote his life to preaching the Jesus he had devoted all his bitter hatred to.

But notice the change from 'I' in v 13, 14 to 'God' in v 15, 16. God had different plans for Paul's life. Only God could have interrupted Paul's vicious career and turned him into His willing apostle. It is just the same for us; our rebellion might have been less active but it takes God's power to break it. *Read Acts 26 v 9 - 23.*

Look at my movements after conversion! (v 17 - 24)

Three years in Arabia, only fifteen days at H.Q in Jerusalem, then fourteen years in Syria and Cilicia (see 2 v 1). Hardly a recipe for indoctrination from the other apostles! In the earlier years at least it appears his only contact with the apostles was a fortnight with Peter and one other apostle in Jerusalem! True, the Judean churches had heard news of his amazing conversion, but to them he was a total stranger. Paul was hardly a key player among them, trained up by the other apostles to preach to the Gentiles!

No, there was no other explanation for Paul's conversion, Paul's apostleship, Paul's gospel. **It all came from God!** Jesus revealed Himself to Paul (v 16), then He revealed His gospel plan to him (v 11, 12). The reaction of the Galatian believers - and our own reaction - should be that of the Judean churches in v 24. Rather than dispute Paul's authority, let's glorify God for so dramatically and conclusively calling him to declare to us the amazing gospel of His grace.

Gospel victory   *Galatians 2 v 1 - 10*

The year AD50 or thereabouts was a crucial one in the early Christian church. The Gentile issue came to a head; would the apostles at Jerusalem give way to pressure from certain Jewish 'Christians' to insist that Gentile Christians should be circumcised according to Old Testament law? (Circumcision was the removal of male foreskin as a mark of belonging to Old Testament Israel.)

A minor point you may think - but why did Paul see it as such a vital issue? *Read v 1 - 10* and the fuller account in *Acts 15 v 1 - 32.* (Though some think this was a different occasion.)

The gospel was at stake! Circumcision itself is neither here nor there, but as soon as **anything** is made a requirement for recognition as a 'real' Christian, it must be resisted tooth and nail. If salvation is not free of entry qualifications it is not salvation at all. The Jerusalem conference was a resounding victory not for Paul but for the gospel.

- **THE APOSTLES WERE UNITED.** Paul need have had no anxiety over the position of the Jerusalem apostles (v 2). Private discussion soon showed they had no intention of compromising with these Judaising so-called-Christians. No, Paul had not run in vain (meaning that so much of his work would have been seriously undermined had Peter and the other apostles given way). They agreed with him completely. But now, as Paul writes a year or two later, these false teachers were still trying to drive a wedge between Paul and the other apostles, to discredit Paul's teaching. But there was no disagreement; Paul's gospel was Peter's gospel.

> The wedge-driving business is still flourishing! Never think of Paul's teaching as any different from Peter's or James' or Jesus'. Different styles, different angles, different audiences - but precisely the same gospel.

- **TITUS WAS NOT CIRCUMCISED.** Paul was a brave man to take along Titus, of pure Gentile extraction! But the test case worked - there was no question of giving in to the demands to have him circumcised (v 3, 5)

> Christians have been set free from slavery - never enslave youself again to man-made regulations that others insist you must keep (v 4).
> Think how this applies in today's churches - it might be subtle!

- **THE GOSPEL WAS ADVANCED** (v 6 - 10). There was no way (as his opponents perhaps suggested) that Paul's gospel had been learnt from or modified by the other apostles - he had been teaching it unsupervised for years! Rather they were able to greatly encourage one another in their separate ministries. Now they could get on with spreading the gospel with full confidence in one another. In addition the fellowship between Jew and Gentile believers would be strengthened by Gentile giving to the poor Jewish churches (v 10).

> Rumours abound. Attempts to discredit preachers are many and varied. Far better to talk to them rather than talk about them! Are they preaching the true gospel? Then let's offer 'the right hand of fellowship' to encourage one another in our different spheres of spreading the gospel.

Standing up to Peter   *Galatians 2 v 11 - 16*

Hypocrite! A title none of us likes to think applies to us, and yet it probably does more times than we would care to admit. Living by your convictions is fine while everyone else agrees with them; it is when they become unpopular that you begin to wish you could be more flexible ...

There was nothing wrong with Peter's convictions about Gentile Christians. He had not so quickly forgotten his Cornelius experience in Acts 10. And the Jerusalem conference was even more recent. Peter knew that in Christ there is neither Jew nor Gentile, but we are all one in Him. It was just that the fear of others' opinions got the better of him -

Read v 11 - 14.

It really had been rather serious; for a key apostle to start voting with his feet and refuse fellowship with Gentile believers was a strong signal to others to fall in line. It would certainly have taken a brave man to remain true to the gospel. Paul was such a man. What is more he was just as much an apostle as Peter, and had the authority as well as the courage to correct Peter publicly. And this is Paul's point here; the Galatian Christians must understand his authority to insist on the truth of the gospel as well as his ability to argue it.

Next time you experience that guilty feeling when your actions deny your beliefs, think what kind of impact it may be having on others. Are unbelievers saying *'If that's all Christianity counts for I want nothing to do with it'*? Are believers saying *'If he/she can do it then it must be all right for me'*?

Though Peter and the others knew they were wrong to refuse to have fellowship with Gentile believers, Paul spells it out.

Read v 14b - 16.
  If God has accepted them, then who are we to reject them!

Even we Jews have given up trying to get right with God by obeying the Law. We trust Jesus Christ now for our salvation. Why ask Gentiles to do something we have learnt to give up?! **Colossians 3 v 11.**

That is the implication of the verses. Christ's free salvation puts all believers on precisely the same level. Are we also guilty of refusing fellowship with any whom Christ has received, perhaps because they do not share our view on secondary issues ...? That is worth thinking through carefully.

This section is probably all part of what Paul had to say to Peter and the others, but it is precisely what the Galatian believers needed to grasp too ...

Read v 15 - 21.

JUSTIFIED BY CHRIST (v 15 - 18)

'Justified' is one of those key New Testament words which all Christians need to master. If it is still vague in your mind invest a few minutes now! Imagine a law court ... the judge is about to pass sentence ... INNOCENT! The person walks free, **justified**, declared innocent. It is the opposite of being condemned. But how can the just Judge of the world justify sinners who are clearly not innocent? Never by our own efforts since we are still guilty of past sins, however much good we may do. Only BY CHRIST. He alone can declare a believer innocent because He has borne the punishment due for his or her sins. He alone can make me right with God, when I have been wrong.

Justified ... declared innocent ... made right with God. With those definitions in mind try to follow Paul's reasoning in *Romans 3 v 20 - 4 v 5.*

The argument in v 17, 18 is difficult. Paul is appealing to Peter: *If while relying on Christ to justify you, you agree with the Judaisers that it is a sin to reject the ceremonial law, then you are actually making Jesus a sin-promoter! (Because He is the One who says trust ME alone, not the works of the law!) No, the transgressor is the one who neglects justification by Christ by rebuilding the system of law-keeping he had abandoned or torn down!*

CRUCIFIED WITH CHRIST (v 19, 20)

It was as if when Jesus died on the cross, Paul's old life of struggling to keep the law's demands died with Him. When Jesus died for his sins, Paul died to the law. Jesus had perfectly satisfied God's standards for Paul by keeping all the law's demands on his behalf. Jesus has done it all - the law is completely useless (and never intended) as a way of being accepted by God!

LIVING BY FAITH IN CHRIST (v 20)

Paul has died, but he is alive! A totally new life has sprung out of the grave of his old law-keeping life. It is a life of trusting the Saviour alone rather than his own works, a life of gratitude for the Saviour's death rather than of confidence in his own achievements. In fact so far has Paul abandoned self that he claims to have no life at all independent of the Saviour, but instead that Christ is the One who lives in him!

Can you see what Paul is driving at in v 21 as he winds up his argument? *I don't ignore God's free grace and go back to trying to earn salvation - if that was possible the cross was a waste.* Either Christ has done everything for our salvation or nothing at all. Either it is all of God's free grace or we are left to our own efforts to satisfy God's holy demands. Look at the headings again - are they true of you? Can you honestly join in with v 20? There is no other way to be saved.

O foolish Galatians!   *Galatians 3 v 1 - 9*

Paul was not one to mince words. Having spent most of the first two chapters establishing his authority as an apostle (and therefore the truth of the gospel he preached), he comes straight to the point - *read v 1 - 9.*

It was not only wrong to take on board this 'Christ + circumcision' gospel - it was sheer stupidity! For two reasons:

1. PAST EXPERIENCE SAYS SO - v 1 - 5.

- **Christ crucified had been displayed to them (v 1).** Their faith had been so clear in the Christ who hung there on the cross, suffering for their sins. They had looked to Him alone to save them. But now it was as if the false teachers had cast a spell on them so they could no longer see the cross ...
- **They had received God's Spirit by faith in Christ.** They knew their faith in Christ had not been misplaced or phoney - because God's Spirit had changed their lives! Gone was the grim, dead routine of law works - now they knew the freedom of Christian living. And, on top of the personal transformation the Spirit had brought were the miracles (perhaps healings or conversions) He had worked (v 5).
- **They had suffered many things for their faith (v 4).** That is how much they believed in Christ ... but now suffering was neatly avoided by compromising with the Judaisers.

Fools! Was there something wrong with trusting Christ alone for salvation, so that now you have to add your own endeavours (v 3)? Was God's gift of the Spirit inadequate for you?!

Never get side-tracked. We can only be saved by beginning with Christ, carrying on with Christ and ending with Christ. Never **assume** you are a Christian because of what happened years ago - if you are not trusting **now** in Christ alone you have no grounds for confidence.

2. THE SCRIPTURE SAYS SO - v 6 - 9.

The force of quoting the example of the Jews' hero Abraham would not be lost on the Galatians. The Jews prided themselves on being the 'sons of Abraham', but his true sons are those who share his faith. Not the Pharisees, not these Judaisers who want to mix Christ with keeping the law, but **Christians**, whether Jew or Gentile, whose faith is in Christ alone to be their righteousness. Like Abraham they are putting their faith in what God has done, not on what they do.

Fools! Are you ignoring the clear teaching of the scriptures? You are one with Abraham himself when you trust in Christ. Don't be conned by these false teachers when their own Old Testament hero is against them!

Never leave the Bible. However attractive the new teaching may be, no other truth but Bible truth can be safe to rely on.

Read Romans 4 v 1 - 25. (Paul proves that circumcision cannot be a requirement for salvation since even Old Testament Abraham received his promise **before** being circumcised.)

One way only   *Galatians 3 v 10 - 14*

They are such nice people, kind and helpful, always willing to help around the church, moral and honest. They imagine God will look favourably on their efforts to lead a good life, that really they are Christians or at least the next best thing ...

Perhaps we even begin to think of them in the same way. We need to look in these verses at Paul's two stark alternative ways to God - to see again there is in fact just one way to receive eternal life. We need to examine our own route - and destiny; is it **law** and **works** leading to **curse**, or is it **promise** and **faith** leading to **blessing**?

Read v 10 - 14.

Route 1; LAW ... WORKS ⇨ CURSE

Verse 10 is so blunt and shocking - and yet so universally true. There is no 'second prize' for those who struggle to please God their own way, only the dreadful curse of His everlasting wrath. Why? Because if they set themselves the task of satisfying God's holy standards they must sinlessly and consistently keep '**all** the things' written in His law (v 10). It is only these (imaginary!) people who find eternal life by this route (v 12). It is perfectly obvious that 'there is none righteous, no not one', that no-one can be right with God by keeping the law (v 11).

Route 1 is no route at all - for it is impossibly difficult. Yet millions are on it, hoping their miserable efforts will somehow be good enough for the perfectly holy God, refusing to believe that His curse not His blessing is upon them. Are you still on this route?

Route 2; PROMISE ... FAITH ⇨ BLESSING

Verse 13 is as shocking as verse 10 - and yet so gloriously true! That Jesus, God's own perfect Son, should come under His curse for us can only leave us in open-mouthed adoring wonder if we but begin to grasp its meaning. And that, in bearing our sins in His own body on the tree, He should set us free from the law's condemnation hanging over us, so that it has no further demand on us!
    Who is it that lives because Jesus died for them?
    Who are justified because Jesus bore the curse of the law for them?
    Who receives the blessing of God's Spirit promised to Abraham?

Find the answer in v 11 and v 14. It is those who have **faith**. It is those who have stopped trusting their law-keeping to gain favour with God. It is those who rely on Jesus alone for eternal life.

Route 2 is the only route for sinners like you and me. There is nothing for me to do - just to trust Christ who has done it all. Then the priceless blessing of God will be mine - for ever. Have you joined this route?

'I have set before you life and death, blessing and cursing: therefore choose life.'

*Read **Deuteronomy 30 v 11 - 20**,* and the new Testament explanation in ***Romans 10 v 1 - 13.***

How the law fits in *Galatians 3 v 15 - 22*

If salvation has always been by faith in God's promise, even as far back as Abraham, where does the law fit in?

Read v 15 - 22.

The law does not CANCEL the promise (v 15 - 18).

Even a human will cannot be cancelled ('anulled', disannulled') or even added to once confirmed by the testator's death. How much less could God say 'I've changed My mind about My promise to Abraham - it is to be replaced by the law!' Neither had God's promise to Abraham already been fulfilled by the time Moses was given the law; that could not possibly be the case because the promise was to **Christ** (v 16). True, the surface meaning was that Abraham's descendants should inherit the land of Canaan, but Abraham knew the promise stretched forwards to Christ, along with all who trust in Him (as indicated by the use of the collective term 'seed' rather than the plural 'descendants' - v 16). See, for example, *Genesis 22 v 17, 18.*

Right through the Old Testament the promise stood. It was **by faith in the promise** that believers were saved, never by obedience to the law of Moses. *Read Hebrews 11 v 13 - 16.*

The law is not AGAINST the promise (v 21).

The ultimate purpose of the law is just that of the promise - salvation! In fact had the law been possible for man to keep, that would have been the result. It is only when people insist that it **is** possible to keep the law to satisfy God, that there is conflict with the promise of free salvation. But, when the law's true purpose is seen, it agrees perfectly with the promise! What is that purpose?...

The law's purpose is to LEAD to the promise (v 19 - 22).

It is hopeless to perfectly keep God's law! As soon as we try we are condemned for our failure and sin. But that was the whole point of introducing the law! To show up our true guilt before God and our helplessness to save ourselves - **so that we would eagerly receive by faith God's promise of free salvation in Jesus.** The law is inferior to the promise, as shown by verse 20*, but it is still necessary for the promise. *Read Romans 3 v 19, 20.*

The law still has its purpose! We are not to jump straight to the good news; we skip over God's holy requirements at the peril of souls. If people have never felt condemned by the law, how can they value being set free from condemnation by the gospel? If they have never seen how hopeless it is for them to please God, how will they come to trust Christ's perfect life and death on their behalf.

---

* Verse 20 is difficult. It seems to show the law's inferiority lies in being given through Moses as a mediator, a third party - while the promise was given directly by God Himself ('God is one')

Which regime?   *Galatians 3 v 23 - 29*

| UNDER LAW | — faith → | IN CHRIST |

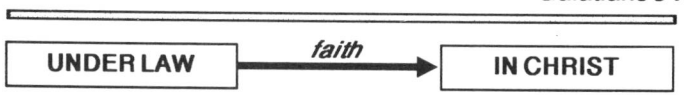

You and I together with the rest of mankind fit in one or other of the two boxes. Each has begun 'UNDER LAW'; obliged to keep God's holy standards. But, as we saw in the last section, the requirements of God's law, formalised in the law given to Moses, point us to Christ. The impossibility of meeting its standards leads us not to despair but to faith in Jesus. As we trust in what He has done we are set free from law's regime; we move from UNDER LAW to IN CHRIST.

Read v 23 - 29.

UNDER LAW   The law's harsh grip on us is described by two vivid illustrations;

- **under guard - v 23.** It is like being in a high-security prison. Guards surround us on all sides; there is no escape from the severe requirements the law places us under.
- **under tutor - v 24.** The term indicates a disciplinarian rather than a teacher; usually a slave whose task it was to make sure a child learnt to keep the rules. The law's rule is one of threats and punishments for those - all of us - who fall short of its demands.

Yet the prison-term is only designed to be temporary! The tutor is only over us until we grow up! The law's harsh regime is only until faith comes! It prepares us by making us long to be set free, and glad to trust ourselves to the Saviour (v 23, 24). Then everything changes ...

IN CHRIST   The contrast has to be experienced to be appreciated;

- **sons of God! - v 26.** Prisoner becomes prince! Jesus not only sets His people free, He brings them into His royal family. Believers are not only made right with God, they come into intimate friendship with Him. Now they are to call the Lord of glory the name that only children can; Abba, Father. This is a Christian's highest privilege; never take it for granted, never be casual about it. *1 John 3 v 1, 2.*
- **one in Christ Jesus! - v 28.** A radically new relationship with God brings a radically new relationship to **all** His children. Think how revolutionary verse 28 would have originally sounded! The differences remain, but they no longer matter in Christ. What matters now is not what used to separate us, but what now unites us - Jesus! *John 17 v 20 - 23.*
- **Abraham's seed! - v 29.** You may sometimes feel lonely and isolated as Christians - but stop to think of the vast multitude you now belong to, the 'sand on the seashore' who are Abraham's promised seed! And, along with each of those like Abraham who believe, you have a destiny to look forward to. Abraham's seed are **heirs**; they will certainly possess the promised land of glory. *Titus 3 v 7.*

It is vital to know whose rule we are under. Do those priceless privileges of those IN CHRIST belong to you? Are you enjoying them? Are you living as sons, brothers and heirs? Or are you still UNDER LAW? Trapped and miserable because you cannot please God ... yet still not willing to have Christ - and freedom.

Once slaves, now sons   *Galatians 4 v 1 - 7*

Paul seems to have reached the climax of his argument at the end of chapter 3; *'The law was never intended as a way to life; its function was to turn people to the promise made to Abraham, that through faith in Christ they would become sons of God and heirs of that promise.'*

The implication is clear; it is spiritual suicide to turn back again to the slavery of law-keeping - if you are sons and heirs, don't go back to being slaves! But, before spelling that out (v 8 onwards), Paul backtracks to make sure we have got the point; *Read v 1 - 7.*

What we were - v 1 - 3.

Slaves. Even though we believers were always destined to be sons and heirs, before God made us heirs we were no better off than slaves. It is just like a child who is the heir of his father's wealth - it makes no difference to him in practice until he is actually given the possession of it. Until God gave us possession of the promise we actually were **slaves** under the law, or as Paul puts it here (v 3), under the elements of the world (meaning man's basic notion of pleasing God by his own efforts). That is how it was in our 'childhood', until God by His grace did something to bring us into full sonship ...

What God did - v 4 - 6.

- **sent His Son into the world.** In His time, when He saw the time was ripe, God acted to rescue His people from their slavery. He sent the only Person who could possibly do this;

  'His Son'; because only God the Son could pay the great redemption price* needed to adopt us **out** of our sins **into** His family (v 5).

  'born of a woman'; **a man,** because only a man could pay the redemption price for man.

  'under the law'; because only by perfectly fulfilling the law we had failed under, could He redeem us from the curse of the law (3 v 13).

- **sent His Spirit into our hearts.** Having acted in His time in the world's history to redeem His sons, He acts in His time by His Spirit in the lives of His sons to bring them into the family! God gave His Son to redeem them and His Spirit to show them they are redeemed. And perhaps the most special and intimate way He does that is to show them they are sons! Not by some remarkable experience, but by the quiet testimony in their hearts that they are right to call God 'Abba, Father'.

  Read Romans 8 v 1 - 17.

Conclusion - v 7.

No longer a slave! A son! An heir! Have you taken hold of the greatness of what God has done for you, if indeed He has? Spend a while going back through the verses in grateful praise. Surely then you will be very quick to resist any requirements that threaten to rob you of these immense privileges and bring you back into slavery ...

*To 'redeem' is to buy back from slavery. Jesus' own blood was the redemption price He paid for Christians.

Birth-pangs - again   *Galatians 4 v 8 - 20*

Paul's next argument is startling to say the least! How dare he compare these sacred Jewish traditions with the idol worship they had turned away from when they became Christians! And yet, when trusted in as a way of becoming acceptable to God, they amount to just the same thing! Yes, these Gentile believers were actually being introduced to a different form of their old heathen practices - to the useless and miserable efforts that enslaved them in the days when they had no knowledge at all of God! *Read v 8 - 11.*

No wonder Paul was afraid for them; if they showed such an appetite for effort-based religion, was it possible they had never truly known the free salvation of Christ? Up to now he has used reason and Bible teaching to persuade them, but now in v 12 he opens his heart and begins to **plead** with them ;

Become like me, trusting only in Christ to save you - because I became like you Gentiles, no longer a Jew trusting in his law-works, but a sinner needing Christ...

Read v 12 - 20.

Once their friend ... (v 12 - 15)

In the past they had done nothing against Paul; (v 12b). Far from it! Despite the fact he had come to them in physical weakness (probably he had been forced to stop in Galatia **because** of illness) in no way had they despised him. In fact they had welcomed him as an angel - a messenger from God - and believed his message as if he had been Christ himself! And that was right; they had recognised his authority as an apostle (a 'sent one' from God), one who was Christ's ambassador. Such was their love and respect for him that they would have done anything for him (v 15). Read how the gospel was first received in Galatia, despite Jewish opposition - *Acts 13 v 42 - 14 v 7.*

Now their enemy? (v 16 - 18)

What has changed? Paul is still telling them the truth just as he always had! Are they being turned against him by these Judaising false teachers? Will they be won by their enthusiastic recruiting? Will they be taken in by their bitter prejudices against Paul? Paul wants the Galatians to know that the great interest these people show for them is only to win them over to their party - to convince them that unless they signed up they would be excluded ('alienate' NIV) from the real thing, the rich blessings of 'true Jewish Christianity'.

This teaching is just that of some thriving cults today. Unless we join up with their system we are poor Christians at best - we are missing out! Beware! They are hungry for new recruits that will be zealous not for the gospel, but for themselves (v 17).

'My little children ... ' (v 19). Paul was really going through it for these Galatians. He had been in labour-pangs for them once already, but now he was agonising all over again for their salvation - as if they needed to be 'born again' again.

Are you causing similar pain and anxiety to those who care for you as their children? Listen to their warnings - they love you!

Isaacs not Ishmaels!   *Galatians 4 v 21 - 31*

Paul has one final approach to take with the Galatians to clinch his argument. They insist on going back to the law? Very well, we will see what the law has to say about it! He uses Old Testament history as a picture, or allegory. The Jews were so proud of being decendants of Abraham, but the key question, according to scripture, is which of his two sons, Isaac or Ishmael, are we the spiritual decendants of?

God had promised Abraham a great multitude of decendants. But his wife Sarah was infertile and far too old. So the birth of the promised son, Isaac, was a miracle, an act of God.

That is like salvation - a miracle from God to make us sons, like Isaac, through faith in His promise.

Read Genesis 21 v 1 - 7.

However Abraham had been impatient. Meanwhile he had a son, Ishmael, by Hagar, Sarah's slave. Ishmael was the slave-son of Abraham's own efforts.

That is like us relying on our law-keeping to save us. It makes us slaves, like Ishmael.

Read Genesis 16 v 1 - 4, 15, 16.

Keeping that basic framework in mind, follow through this difficult section - *v 21 - 28*. The diagram below may help.

```
                        ABRAHAM
          ←──────────────┼──────────────→
  ┌─────────────────────┐   ┌─────────────────────┐
  │ SARAH represents ...│   │ HAGAR represents ...│
  └─────────────────────┘   └─────────────────────┘
  NEW COVENANT - promise      OLD COVENANT - works
  JERUSALEM ABOVE - Christian church   MT SINAI - law
  FREEDOM                     EARTHLY JERUSALEM - Jews
                              SLAVERY
            ↓                           ↓
  ┌─────────────────────┐   ┌─────────────────────┐
  │    ISAAC - SON      │   │   ISHMAEL - SLAVE   │
  └─────────────────────┘   └─────────────────────┘
```

Now you, Galatian believer, are an Isaac, not an Ishmael (v 28)! It is no use struggling to be a son of Abraham by your own law-observance - that makes you an Ishmael, a slave. You are the spiritual son of Abraham by faith in God's promise. You belong not to the family of Jews but to Jerusalem above, the family of believers.

And, as an Isaac, you must expect the treatment true sons receive from their half-brothers ... *Read Genesis 21 v 8 - 12 and Galatians 4 v 28 - 31.*

Often it is not the irreligious but the very religious that most bitterly attack Christians. The Ishmaels, who are enraged to be told that their religious deeds will not save them. But it is vital not to compromise and so duck out of the persecution, like the Galatians were being tempted to do - why?

         v 30 - there is no place in heaven for slave-children.

Circumcision or Christ   *Galatians 5 v 1 - 6*

Stand firm! Do not give an inch to those who want to burden you down like an ox carrying a yoke. Christ has set you free from one slavery, heathenism; do not exchange your freedom for another set of rules and rituals. (Compare with *Matthew 23 v 2, 4*)

Read v 1.

But Paul, some might have said, *you are carrying this too far! We have no intention of leaving our faith in Christ in favour of Jewish ceremonialism. There are just one or two Old Testament practices (such as circumcision) that we are being taught are necessary **on top of** trusting Christ's salvation. Surely that is not the massive problem you make it out to be...?*

Paul is anxious to knock any such thinking on the head. He deliberately speaks as forcefully and clearly as he knows how; *read v 2 - 4.*

CIRCUMCISION or CHRIST
LAW or GRACE

It is impossible to mix them - they are incompatible. Either you rest entirely on what Christ has done, or you are left to trust entirely on what you can do. Either salvation comes freely by God's gift of undeserved grace, or you must earn it by your law-keeping. To put it simply, either Christ is your Saviour, or you must save yourself - you cannot have it both ways. As soon as you accept a single requirement on top of faith in Christ, you have deserted Christ. You are on your own; you must perfectly keep the whole of God's holy law.

Besides, circumcision was the sign of the Old Covenant! To be circumcised was to bind yourself to the Jewish religion. In effect it was saying that Christians need to be Jews.

Never conclude that we or others are all right so long as we have faith in Christ. If we are 'topping up' faith in Christ by trusting in our own effort or devoutness, we have 'fallen from grace'. Those who think they have Christ + religious observance, or Christ + good works in reality are severed from Christ altogether.

Circumcision must be an irrelevance to a Christian, because it has nothing to do with salvation. It counts for nothing. But what does count? How do Christians live if it is not by law-observance?

Read v 5, 6.

BY FAITH!
- **Faith that waits for salvation, not works for it (v 5).** Do you have an **eager expectation** of God pronouncing you righteous, and welcoming you into heaven? That is from God's Spirit working faith in you; such a faith is based on what Jesus has done, not from faith in our own works.
- **Faith that works by loving (v 6).** We are saved by faith, not works - but faith always works! That is how we can tell if faith is genuine; it produces love. Love for Christ, love for Christian brothers and sisters, love even for our enemies. Does your faith work?

Read James 2 v 14 - 26.

Who hindered you?   *Galatians 5 v 7 - 15*

The Galatians had started the Christian race fine, they were running strongly with their eyes fixed on Jesus. But now who had put this obstacle in the track?

Read v 7 - 12.

- Certainly not people who were sent from the Master (v 8). The Saviour had called them by His grace and still urges them onwards; this circumcision teaching was foreign to the gospel that had saved them, from an intruder who would stop them running the race.
- People who were causing a lot of damage (v 9, 10). Like leaven, a little bad teaching can go a long way. Just a few of these false teachers were disrupting most if not all of the churches in Galatia.
- People who must face God's judgement for their actions (v 10). Paul was convinced that the Galatians would come to their senses; nevertheless the false teachers would in the end pay for the damage they had done.

These people might throw Paul's accusations back in his face and say that he taught circumcision himself when it suited him. But Paul's insistence that the Gentiles should not be circumcised was the very thing that he had suffered so much for. If only he had compromised with the Jews and taught the necessity of Christians observing Jewish customs then he could have avoided so much persecution. It was the teaching of salvation by the cross of Christ **alone** that was so offensive (v 11).

No, not Paul but these teachers of circumcision were threatening to wreck the churches. How Paul longed for them to disappear, to as it were do the operation on themselves and go the whole way - to cut themselves off completely from the churches (v 12)!

The false teachers had certainly caused damage, but Paul adds a word of warning to the Christians lest they should do even more damage to each other -

Read v 13 - 15.

Stand firm in your liberty (v 1), but do not use it to attack each other! Remember that Christ has set you free not so you can indulge your passions which love to argue - but to be willing, loving slaves of each other! He has set you free from the law's demands - so you can gladly obey its commands! Out of gratitude for Christ you will want to 'love your neighbour as yourself' and so fulfil the law.

Read Romans 13 v 8 - 10; 1 Corinthians 10 v 23, 24, 31 - 33.

How much dispute among Christians would be resolved if only we kept the law of love? In standing for the truths we love, do we trample over the people we should love? Let us fight for the doctrine of 'salvation by grace through faith alone' - but not then contradict it by fighting God's people rather than the error that has deceived them!

Spirit vs flesh *Galatians 5 v 16 - 21*

Have you discovered how impossible it is to get the better of your sinful nature by your own efforts? You may have struggled long and hard to defeat those sinful desires, as those 'under the law', but to no avail. ('Lust' in the Bible refers not only to sexual passion, but any strong desire - normally sinful.)

'Under the law' our struggle against sin is a miserable failure; but how can **Christians** defeat their inbred passion for sin?

Read v 16 - 18.

BY THE SPIRIT

God's Holy Spirit is stronger than our sinful desires! If He is **leading** us (v 18) to do the things which please God and we are responding by **walking** by His directions (v 16) then we **cannot** at the same time gratify the desires of our old nature!

BY A LIFELONG STRUGGLE

The battle is on! In every believer there is a tug-of-war between the Spirit and the 'flesh' (our old sinful nature). The Spirit has taken control of his life, but the flesh will fight to the bitter end to regain its place. Final victory belongs to the Spirit, but the flesh wins a lot of skirmishes; far too often we succumb to its enticements and fall into the sin we really hate. The way to fight is not to go back to rigid law-keeping, but by living under the Spirit's control. *Read Romans 7 v 15 - 25.*

How ashamed we should be when we come to specifics and see just what evils we can give way to. Listen to the flesh and you will let a flood of foul sin into your life ...

Read v 19 - 21. (Use a dictionary if you need to!)
- **Sexual sins (v 19).** How appropriate to present society that these should come first! It is foolhardy to imagine that we are strong enough to stand firm when the world is screaming at us 'do it if it feels good'. Saturate yourself with what the Spirit says, ruthlessly avoid any situation that triggers off impure thoughts, ask the Lord to keep you firm.
- **Religious sins (v 20).** It may seem strange that in a godless age false religion and witchcraft thrive - but the truth is that the 'flesh' is very religious.
- **Social sins (v 20, 21).** Eight or nine evils springing from **me** mattering more than **you**. If love fulfills the law, then the absence of love for others leads to every evil imaginable in the way we treat them. Let the list search you.
- **Sins of excess (v 21).** Self-control is a key New Testament virtue - but one considered of minor importance today. 'Letting yourself go' is letting go of the Spirit and letting the flesh have a free hand. The last two in the list are two shameful examples of the consequences.

'Walk in the Spirit' and you will not live like this. Yes, Christians may and do slip into even the worst of these sins - but do not be deceived; if this list continues to **characterise** your life the 'flesh' is still in control. *Read v 21 again.*

The fruit of the Spirit   *Galatians 5 v 22 - 25*

If the works of the flesh no longer characterise a believer's life, then what does?

Read v 22, 23.

If we do not have this fruit we cannot have the Spirit! The Spirit always produces fruit, more or less, in believers. And, what is more, it will always have all nine characteristics, more or less. Notice it is not nine different **fruits** (of which we may have two or three)- it is nine different things about one **fruit** (which will always be true of it).

Love ... joy ... peace.	Mainly to do with **relationship with God**. We cannot be very fruitful Christians unless our relationship with God is right. We may be very likable, very cheerful, very friendly, but not very **Christlike** if we have grown distant from our God. It is when our chief love is love for God, our greatest joy the joy of knowing the Lord and our deepest peace knowing the Saviour's smile upon us, that we really start to be of use to the Lord and to others. Is this growing in closeness to the Lord your priority?
Longsuffering ... kindness ... goodness.	To do with **relationship with others**. This is putting into practice what God is towards us! It is putting up with a lot from people without rejecting them or hitting back ... looking out for ways of showing love to people in need ... doing and saying good things to people whether or not they deserve it.
Faithfulness ... gentleness ... self-control.	Faithfulness towards God; sticking to His Word, His commands, His people. Gentleness towards others; being sensitive to their feelings, accepting it when they are insensitive to ours. Self-control towards ourselves! Mastering our desires, our reactions, our words.

Even such a brief glance at the two contrasting lists will leave Christians saying; *'How can I be rid of the works of the flesh and show more of the fruit of the Spirit?* -

Read v 24, 25.
- **By remembering you have crucified the lusts of the flesh!** You are united to Christ in His crucifixion. As He died **for** your sin, so you died **to** your sin. It was nailed to a cross, defeated. You have turned your back on it, you have said you will have nothing more to do with it. **So live like that!** Don't be tempted to resurrect those sins you once left on the cross! *(Romans 6 v 6)*
- **By walking in the Spirit!** Just as decisively as we reject what is sinful, we must go for what is good. If the Spirit really is living in us, then we must wholeheartedly respond to His instruction. We must 'keep in step' with Him, not lagging behind, but eagerly looking to please Him. *Romans 6 v 13* sums it up.

Now try to follow Paul's reasoning in that chapter; *Romans 6 v 6 - 23.*

One another   *Galatians 5 v 26 - 6 v 5*

Spiritual people are not proud of their spirituality! Yet don't you find that, particularly when others are falling into some error or some sin, it is all too easy for that superior feeling to creep in? Paul teaches us how **not** to react and how **to** react in such a situation.

Read the section.

Wrong approach to others - SUPERIORITY.

'One another' is a key phrase in this section. We are not to look on each other as the competition to get the better of - but as fellow-believers to help on the way together!

- **No conceit!** (5 v 26, 6 v 3) *Who makes you to differ from another?* Paul asks of the Corinthian believers, *What do you possess that you did not first receive as a gift from God? Read 1 Corinthians 4 v 5 - 8.*
  When we were first saved we knew we were nothing (6 v 3); has that changed ...?
- **No provoking!** (5 v 26) No challenging others to prove that we know best. No asserting ourselves to show who is on top.
- **No envying!** (5 v 26) We may not actually feel superior ... **but is that what we want to be!** It is really the same attitude; just as wrong, just as damaging.
- **No comparing!** (6 v 4, 5) We can always make ourselves feel good by looking for others who are not doing so well. But God is not interested in how we compare with Jane or Jimmy; His question is how we match up to His own standards set out in the Bible. We had better start examining ourselves in that light before we start boasting to ourselves. Others will have to answer to the Lord for their lives, but our business is to be sure we can face Him with a good conscience (v 5).

Right approach to others - BURDEN-SHARING.

Where they are in comparison to us on the spiritual league table is irrelevant. In fact we are no longer thinking in terms of position - our only concern is to help our brothers and sisters grow more holy and useful. So what is our response to a believer who has begun to accept false teaching (like these Galatians), or given way to some sin that has caught him unawares ('overtaken')?

- **Restore him!** (v 1) That is the spiritual person's desire - to rescue him from whatever it is that is threatening his Christian life and usefulness. He will not immediately 'spread the news' but stop and pray over what he can do to help his brother or sister.
- **Be gentle!** ('meek' A.V - v 1) Some people love to get out their surgeon's scalpel and 'sort out' other people's problems. But the attitude of one who knows that but for God's grace it could have been him, is very tender and sensitive.
- **Bear the burden!** (v 2) God has given us one another to help us through times of weakness - let us keep His law of love! *Read Romans 15 v 1 - 7.*

Verses 2 and 5 are complimentary not contradictory! Remember their lessons: **Don't be superior** towards others; make sure your own life is right, for that is what God will hold you responsible for (v 5). Instead, **share one another's burdens** when they are weak; for this is the way to live right according to Christ's law of love (v 2).

Reaping what you sow   *Galatians 6 v 6 - 10*

As Paul nears the end of his letter there are a few other issues he wants to mention. All to do with **reaping what you sow** ...

Read v 6 - 10.

Verse 7 states the principle. If you sow carrots you reap carrots. If you sow lots of carrots you reap lots of carrots! It is so obvious, and yet many of us seem to think that if we sow little or nothing we can still hope for a good harvest. Or worse, that even if we spend our lives sowing thistles, somehow in the end there will be a fine row of carrots to dig ...

We might fool ourselves, but God is not fooled. He sees just what we are sowing and will see to it that we reap just the appropriate harvest.

Now for three examples of the principle applied to our lives:

1. Sow generously to Christian teachers (v 6)

To put it bluntly that means digging into our pockets! If we value the Word as we claim to, it is a strange contradiction when those who preach the Word to us have to scratch around to make ends meet ...

On the other side, ministers should see to it that they sow the Word plentifully; that they are **labourers**, worthy of their wages (Luke 10 v 7). *Read 1 Corinthians 9 v 9 - 14.*

2. Sow to the flesh, reap corruption. Sow to the Spirit, reap everlasting life (v 8)

It is not only the **good** seed that yields a harvest. We all know that weeds not only grow faster than our plants, but also multiply rapidly to cover the whole garden. Yet strangely many Christians seem to imagine they can 'sow to the flesh' as much as they please without reaping any ill effects! Will you indulge in hours of mindless T.V, or feed hungrily on God's Word? Entertain impure fantasy, or set your mind on things above? Will you hang around in dubious company, or fellowship with believers? Laze in bed, or get up to pray?

The question really is this; what do you want to reap? Then sow **those** seeds ...

3. Sow good deeds, reap good results (v 9, 10)

We are not told what exactly will be the harvest that comes from our acts of kindness and love. Often we never know the tremendous good resulting from our stopping to sow a tiny seed. In fact it can be very disheartening when we spend time and effort that seems to achieve little. Perhaps that is why we are exhorted not to give up. No, we should not expect to reap a crop immediately! We are not to be like a child who gives up gardening because his seeds did not spring up overnight.

Instead we should keep sowing as much seed as we can because we are sure that God will keep His promise of a good harvest. *Read 2 Corinthians 9 v 6.*

Cross not Circumcision　　　　　　　　　　　　　　　　　*Galatians 6 v 11 - 18*

It was Paul's custom to have a scribe write down the bulk of a letter for him, and to add the final greeting in his own hand. In this letter he takes the pen a little early and writes a conclusion in large bold letters - probably for emphasis (rather than a large epistle (A.V)).

Read v 11 - 18.

CROSS not CIRCUMCISION

That is what it boiled down to. Let the Jews boast in their circumcision, but the mark of the Christian is to be the cross. The cross of Christ, with all its suffering and humiliation, is the only thing for Christians to boast in!

What, in practice, are the consequences of that?

- **God's new creation** not **man's law-keeping** (v 15 & 13)

  The cross cuts us down to size. It tells us that we are sinners who need a crucified Jesus to save us. It tells us we can do nothing to satisfy God, but must throw ourselves on the mercy of a Saviour who has done everything. It tells us that all our efforts at outward law-keeping are in vain, because first we need an inward transformation. It tells us that we must be new-created, born again, so that we stop trusting our own works and cling to the cross of Christ.

  The old hymn puts it well:　　*'Nothing in my hand I bring*
  　　　　　　　　　　　　　　　　Simply to thy cross I cling'

  That is why the cross is so offensive. It hurts us where it hurts most - our pride.

- **Finishing with the world** not **boasting to the world** (v 14 & 12, 13)

  The cross cuts us off from the world. Not altogether, but in the sense that we no longer belong to it, but to Christ. There has been a double crucifixion; we have done with the world, and the world has done with us; we have nailed all those passions and indulgings to the cross, and in return the world has nailed us up for its scorn and ridicule.

  What a contrast to those who are in it for their own ego! They are out to impress the world not be persecuted by it (v 12)! They are interested in the externals, the things that others can see, not the internals that only God observes. They will boast in the numbers who have been circumcised, or baptised, or come forward in their meetings, or been 'healed' - not in the cross of Christ. *Read 1 John 4 v 4 - 6.*

Can you look verse 14 in the face? What are its implications for your present attitudes and lifestyle?

Now read again v 16 - 18.

It is those who live by the rule of the CROSS not CIRCUMCISION who will know the **peace** of sins forgiven. It is only this true, spiritual 'Israel' who will receive God's **mercy** rather than His wrath. Let those who wear the badge of CIRCUMCISION trouble Paul (and by implication the Galatian believers) no more; for they have no part with him whose very scars show he belongs to the CROSS. *Read 1 Corinthians 1 v 17, 18, 23, 24.*

Do you belong to the cross? *The grace of our Lord Jesus Christ be with your spirit.'*

OUTLINE: Galatians - no additions!

'For in Christ Jesus neither circumcision or uncircumcision avails anything, but faith working through love.' (5 v 6)

- Sum up each section in a short sentence or phrase (ideas below).
- Look for key words in each section (usually repeated).

SECTION	SUMMARY	KEYWORDS
1 v 1 - 5 v 6 - 10 v 11 - 24		
2 v 1 - 10 v 11 - 21		
3 v 1 - 9 v 10 - 14 v 15 - 25 v 26 - 29		
4 v 1 - 7 v 8 - 20 v 21 - 31		
5 v 1 - 67 v 7 - 15 v 16 - 26		
6 v 1 - 5 v 6 - 10 v 11 - 15 v 16 - 18		

glorying in the cross not the flesh ... liberty means love ... sons of Abraham - by faith ... sharing, not superior ... all sons, in Christ ... no other gospel ... standing up to Peter ... redeemed from the curse of the law ... Christ or circumcision ... once a friend, now an enemy? ... the law to bring us to Chist ... gospel victory at Jerusalem ... no longer slaves ... Spirit vs flesh ... blessing ... reaping what we sow ... Isaacs not Ishmaels ... greeting ... revealed directly to Paul ...

FACT - FILE : *Ephesians*

> **EPHESIANS**
>
> Christ and His body

THE CHURCH

- Ephesus was the capital of the Roman province of Asia and a busy commercial port. It was also a major centre of idolatry, notably of the goddess 'Diana of the Ephesians'. See map on page 158.
- The Church there was founded by Paul on his second missionary journey, around AD54 (Acts 19). He stayed at Ephesus for three years, reaching out into all the surrounding area.
- The church was formed from a mixture of Jewish and Greek believers.

THE LETTER

- The author is the apostle Paul, writing from Rome from his house-prison.
- Written around AD62, to the still fairly young church at Ephesus (and probably intended for those in the surrounding region).
- Written at the same time as Paul's letter to the Colossians, there are many resemblances; yet the specific warning about heresies which influences the whole of the Colossian letter is absent from Ephesians.
- Written to stir appreciation and praise for all the blessings believers have in Christ, equally for Jew and Gentile, and so to promote **unity** and **purity** in their lives and relationships.
- Chapters 1 - 3 explore the depths of what Christ has done to bring His people into one body.

    Chapters 4 - 6 show how that one body is to work in practice (in church unity, daily living, family relationships).
- See fuller outline at the end of the section.

If at all possible ...

Find time to read the letter through in one sitting, with this background in mind.

Blessings in Christ   *Ephesians 1 v 1 - 6*

Perhaps we tend to skip over the opening greetings of Paul's letters as if he had not really begun yet. Ours is the loss. *Verses 1, 2* admittedly sound pretty standard, yet they contain keywords that neatly sum up the whole letter:

>God's **grace** bringing us into **peace** with Him, through **Jesus Christ**.

Paul then takes a deep breath and launches into praise. That must be our starting point too if we want to appreciate this glorious letter; lost in wonder love and praise at what God has done for His people through His Son.

Read v 3 - 6 - slowly!

THE BLESSINGS

Having read it, can you respond to it? Pick out the 'spiritual blessings' God has given us in Jesus and spend a while in awe and praise (You will need to go through to v 14!).

Now home in on two of the most glorious yet most undervalued of these blessings;

- *Chosen ... to be holy.* (v 4) It is a tragedy when we reject or ignore what the Bible says because we do not much like the implications. Paul was in love with this truth of election because he loved the implications! He revelled in the total security that comes from being engraved in God's heart before ever we had any say in the matter. He was thrilled at the prospect of being made perfectly holy and free from all blame. Perhaps those who claim that election encourages careless living have not read this verse ...?
- *Predestined ... to be sons.* (v 5) What is the highest privilege a person could ever have? To be a child of God Himself! But if you are a Christian it is not because God made a snap decision to adopt you on that moment you believed! From before the world began He saw you as His child. Throughout your life He watched over you, planning all events to bring you into relationship with your Father.

THE BASIS

'Ah yes', say some, *'God chose us because He saw we would believe. Predestination is on the basis of our choosing Christ.'* Verse 5 cuts right through such confused, unbiblical thinking. What moved God to choose me? Simply His own pleasure, His sovereign will! Praise God that my salvation has a more certain basis than my own changeable, sin-bent will!

THE GOAL

I hope God has stirred your heart to praise Him for these blessings God has purposed for believers in Jesus. But if my praise stops at what God has done for me, doesn't it become self-centred? Verse 6 puts us right. Why, God's ultimate goal was not to save me but to bring praise and glory to His name! Does that not thrill you more than anything else?

Paul starts at the same place in Romans 8. v39 is only for those in v 29! *Read v 28 - 39.*

Salvation - God's eternal purpose   *Ephesians 1 v 7 - 14*

Since we interrupted Paul in mid-flow, perhaps we should go back to the beginning of his sentence and read to the end - *read v 3 - 14* (originally a single sentence!)
Space only permits us to dip into these amazing verses; we will pursue three key themes to whet your appetite to dig more deeply.

1. The Father, the Son, the Holy Spirit.

Are you clear about the part each Person of the Trinity plays in our salvation? Scan these verses and you will be left in little doubt! The Father **took the initiative** (notice all the things which 'He' has done), the Son is the **way of salvation** (count up all the 'in Him's!), the Spirit **brings us to salvation** (the blessings are all 'spiritual' (v 3); God's Spirit brings them to our spirits).

Although the Spirit's work is assumed rather than spelt out for most of the section, one aspect is specifically highlighted at the end - *read v 13, 14*. This is no mystical second blessing belonging only to some. **All** who believe have the Holy Spirit as a **seal** and a **deposit**. The Holy Spirit in their hearts marks them out as belonging to God. But not only that; this presence is a kind of down-payment which guarantees that the rest of the inheritance will follow. It gives us certainty that we are Jesus' 'possession', purchased by His blood; the ones He will come to fetch into heaven.

2. The past, the present, the future.

It sounds stunningly obvious to say that the present is just a speck sandwiched between an eternal past and an eternal future. But it is all too easy to become so 'here-and-now' orientated that we lose that perspective. Unless we can stretch our minds into eternity our praise for salvation will be so weak and cramped; it is worth reading the verses through again to see how Paul's praise spans eternity.

Now with your 'eternity glasses' firmly in place, it would be good to spend a while in grateful praise for some of the **present** blessings; how important it is that a believer's praise is not limited to the same one or two favourites!

- Redemption; Christ paid the price of His own precious blood to purchase **me** for Himself! (v 7)
- Grace; lavished freely, undeservedly on me to forgive every one of my sins. (v 7, 8)
- Communication; He brought us to know for ourselves the 'mystery' of the gospel (v 9)
- Christ; how that in God's chosen time (v 10) He brought everything under Christ's rule; both the creation, His universe, and the new creation, His Church.

3. The will, the activity, the glory.

Man loves to be in control of his own salvation! Emphasise only that he must choose, that he must act - and often he will be happy to 'decide for Christ'. Man's will ... man's activity... so does man get the glory? It is worth a final scan over these verses to notice what thrills Paul about salvation. They are packed with praise for **God's** eternal purposes and for **Christ's** redeeming activity. And who gets the glory then? (v 6, 12, 14)

Of course man's will is involved. Of course he must be active in believing in Christ - but let's join Paul in putting the emphasis back where it belongs.

'that you may know ...'   *Ephesians 1 v 15 - 19*

Have you got your praise and prayer in the right balance? Having blessed God for all the blessings He has for Christians, what comes next? Prayer that they will **know** these blessings that already belong to them in Jesus!

Read v 15 - 19.

The natural reaction is to pray this beautiful prayer for ourselves - and please do! But Paul was actually praying for others. We can pray for one another's health and work and relationships - but above all let's make the spiritual growth of other believers a priority in our prayers. Especially we need to watch over young believers, mixing thanksgiving for their salvation with prayer that they will know Christ more and more (v 15 - 17).

Knowledge. This is what Paul's prayer boils down to. Some people emphasise special experiences, but the only way to **experience** the truth is first to **understand** it. Paul means both when he prays for knowledge. This knowledge is the key to our whole Christian life. The only way to grow, the only way to be useful to God, to be holy, is to grasp hold of the truths of the Bible.

Because ultimately knowledge is to know God Himself, it does not come from sitting with a pile of books. That is why Paul is **praying** for it! Though books may help, the Holy Spirit is essential. He is the 'Spirit of wisdom and revelation' of v 17, who lights up our minds so that it makes sense to us (v 18). And not only does He light us up, He warms us up too.

Knowledge of what in particular? *Read v 18, 19 again.*

- **the hope of His calling.** What were your expectations when you were saved? What promises did He call you to enjoy? You were called to be holy, to freedom from sin, to fellowship with God's people ... ultimately to live with Christ for ever in glory. These are the things we need to grasp hold of.
- **the riches of the glory of His inheritance.** We need to learn to keep our eyes on the prize. We need to do our sums right when faced with pressure and pain and persecution, and despise them in comparison with that eternal weight of glory beckoning us on. *2 Corinthians 4 v 16 - 18.*
- **the exceeding greatness of His power.** Why do we need to understand His power? Because between calling and inheritance comes conflict! And very quickly you begin to see that the power you need must be 'exceedingly great' if ever you are to lay hold of the hopes of the first point.
It **is** exceedingly great. And that is what Paul expands on in the verses we will look at tomorrow ...

But for now we need to put the verses into practice. To pray for ourselves, other individuals, other groups of believers. And to make this prayer for knowledge not a one-off, but a regular feature of our praying. Like Paul did; *Philippians 1 v 9, 10; Colossians 1 v 9, 10.*

The exceeding greatness of His power *Ephesians 1 v 19 - 23*

Crushed under a sense of failure and sin ... shattered by some bitter disappointment ... weary of the constant demand of time and energy ... disillusioned by the lack of success in witness ...

What do we need a constant supply of? Power! Not our own, for that very soon lets us down, but a power that is always available, that meets every situation, defeats any opposition, conquers any sin.

This is just the power Paul is praying his readers will know the 'exceeding greatness' of;

Read v 15 - 23.

- **The power that raised Jesus - v 20.**
  Power which raised the Saviour of sinners to be Conqueror over sin, hell and the devil must be the greatest power in the universe - infinite power. Surely believers can trust such power not only to see them through the conflicts of this life, but to raise **them** together with Christ, victorious over sin!

- **The power of the King of the universe - v 20 - 22.**
  All things under Him - you can't get much more than that! Nothing in all creation, no man, no power, no devil, can act independently of the reigning Christ. *Psalm 8* has had its fulfilment in the perfect Man; join in the psalmist's praise to the Lord of glory as you read it (notice how v 6 is quoted in Ephesians 1 v 22).

There can surely be no remaining doubt; such infinite power is enough for us! But there is something even more special in these verses ...

*'the exceeding greatness of His power **toward us who believe**'* (v 19) ...
*'head over all things **to the church**'* (v 22)!

Not only is His power infinitely great - it is specially for us who believe! He exercises His power over the universe specifically to benefit His church! In fact this power is ...

- **The power of the Head of the church - v 23.**
  Not only Head over the universe for the benefit of the church, but Head over the church itself, His own body. That is how closely He is connected to His people, that is how much He cares for them! Christ fills all the universe in all respects, and yet so intimately connected is He to His people that He counts Himself incomplete without them. They are His 'fullness', His complement without whom He cannot be satisfied.

No wonder Paul prays for a knowledge of this power! Because it is infallible power. Power that cannot let us down in all life's struggles and pressures. Power that is certain to bring every single person who trusts in Christ to possess his inheritance with Christ for ever.

Intolerable or glorious? *Ephesians 2 v 1 - 7*

If ever we are to be saved we need to face the truth of what we are like in the first place. If ever we are to evangelise those around us, we need to be honest in painting a true picture of them.

Paul's description is devastatingly clear - *read v 1 - 3.*

- *DEAD!* (v 1) Not terribly flattering or hopeful. Dead people can't actually do a lot for themselves. It is not that our spiritual life needs stirring into healthy activity - there is none to stir. We have zero love for God, zero response to His Word, zero desire for His glory. Yes we are alive and kicking, but in a different realm altogether - in fact a realm that is totally opposed to spiritual life. We are immersed in a life of rebellion against God ('trespasses') and complete failure to please Him ('sins').

- *ENSLAVED!* (v 2) Let's dispel the myth that people are free to be their own men. If God's Spirit is not in them then Satan's is. And he is busy at work shepherding them down the wide road that leads to destruction. The world blindly follows, without a thought of whose idea it was ...

- *CONDEMNED!* (v3) *'By nature children of wrath'* is a particularly chilling description. Even more so when we notice there is no escape clause; **all** of us were included in this condemnation. Sin and rebellion is in our genes as it were; we are natural sinners because sin is in our constitution. And therefore we are inevitably under God's holy, active, abhorrent anger against sin.
Read Romans 5 v 12 - 14, 18.

Intolerable message? Certainly - unless you read on ... *read v 4 - 7.*

'BUT GOD' cuts through all the helpless misery and despair of v 1 - 3.
- Condemned under God's wrath BUT GOD loved us with great love!
- Enslaved and helpless under Satan's rule BUT GOD had rich mercy on us!
- Dead in our sins BUT GOD made us alive in Christ!

For Christians the intolerable message becomes part of the most glorious message in the world! Those who accept the ugly, inescapable truth about themselves can sing out what God has done to turn all that on its head.

And notice that the BUT GOD says more than 'God has done the impossible for you.' He has not only **cancelled** the curse of v 1 - 3; in His amazing grace He has **replaced** it with the glories of v 5 - 7!

Risen! Ascended! Enthroned! Who, Jesus? No, that was in *chapter 1 v 20 - 23!* Now Paul is describing those of us who have been saved. 'Together with Christ' because He has saved us to be inseparably His. To enjoy **from now on** for ever ('in the ages to come') the oceans of God's free blessings (v 7).

Salvation unlocks the door to God's treasure house - how much have you dared ask Him for?

Do you believe *Romans 8 v 32?*

Grace - free and undeserved *Ephesians 2 v 8 - 13*

'Rich in mercy ... great love ... exceeding riches of His grace ... kindness. Paul has been multiplying words in this chapter to describe God's amazing attitude to rebels dead in their sins.

But **grace** is the one he comes back to in v 8. The more layers of my own sin I discover, the more I love this word 'grace'.

> GRACE is ...   God's free gift of love when I deserved anger.
> God's free gift of forgiveness when I deserved judgement.
> God's free gift of life when I deserved death.
> God's free gift of heaven when I deserved hell.

Now read v 8 - 10.

Grace means no boasting! It was no work of ours that saved us - but Christ's alone (v9). The only part we played was to put our trust in Christ to save us; and even that faith came as a gift from God!

Have you ever noticed a superior feeling creeping in when you are with an unbeliever? Run to these verses! Confess your sin and ask God to show you His amazing grace again.

'Not **of** works lest any should boast' - but **for** works that God should be glorified (v10)! He has handmade His people, created them out of nothing, for a purpose. He has not designed them fixed in a sitting position, but to be real working Christians, 'walking' in the ways He has planned for them. Is your life full of the good works God purposed it to be?

So far Paul has included everyone. But now as a bridge to the following verses he singles out the Gentiles.

Read v 11 - 13.

You were ... (v 11, 12)
The bitter mockery of the Jews (the 'Circumcision') was painfully accurate. Before Christ came the Gentiles were indeed outsiders; having no place in God's kingdom or covenant, no hope (that they knew of) of a coming Saviour, no God (since they had turned to idols).

But now ... (v 13)
What a contrast! Hopelessness, alienation, distance, replaced by the intimate relationship with God that comes from being in Christ.

How we should praise God if the blood of Christ has spanned that vast gulf our sins had made between us and God! Brought near by His free grace!

Read Romans 3 v 21 - 31.

Double peace   *Ephesians 2 v 14 - 22*

Double alienation for the Gentiles: Hostility with God, hostility with the Jews. What dealt with both?

Christ our peace! *Read v 14 - 18.*

- **Peace with Jews (v 14, 15).** The wall surrounding the temple symbolised how the Jews felt towards Gentiles. Warning notices made sure no-one could miss the point; *Gentiles keep out!* Jesus could let the Romans deal with the symbolic barrrier in AD 70; His work was to tear down the real source of hostility -

the law with its commandments and ceremonies.

The law was given to the Jews, not the Gentiles. So far as the Jews were concerned it said 'Gentiles, keep out!' But Christ has abolished the law's demands by fulfilling them! The moral part of the law still holds as God's perfect standard for us all, but law-keeping is ruled out **as the way to God.**

- **Peace with God (v 16).** Jews and Gentiles are now on an equal footing! Both must come to God in just the same way - 'through the cross'. The cross has put to death the hostility between God and repenting sinners! The cross has put to death the hostility between Christian Jew and Gentile!
- **Peace preached. (v 17, 18).** Jesus did not only make peace, He declared it. Through His church Jesus saw to it that Gentiles ('afar off') as well as Jews ('near') should hear the good news; that both Jews and Gentiles should understand they have equally free access to the Father, because it is Christ alone who has made their peace. *Read Romans 5 v 1, 2.*

'Now therefore' says Paul, *'You need to put behind you all the barriers which once separated you, and remember that Gentiles just as much as Jews share enormous privileges in Christ's church'* -

Read v 19 - 22.

Paul is anxious to stress how fully the Gentiles now **belong** in the church. In stark contrast to the alienation of the past, now they are ...

citizens belonging to God's kingdom ... members of God's family ... built into God's temple.

It is the last picture Paul enlarges on, perhaps because it best illustrates equality and inter-relation. The stones are much of a muchness and they must all fit together, whatever their background. The vital thing is to be in the right relationship to the Chief corner stone. For if He controls us we are sure to be growing in a right relationship to all the other stones. That is what it means to be the 'holy temple' that God Himself has come to inhabit ...

Has peace with Christ led in your life to peace with all other true Christians, whatever nationality, class, background or age? Are you part of a holy temple that is growing **together**, fitting closely with all kinds of 'stones'? If not, how does that square with the 'one new humanity' of v 15, which Christ has made through the cross?

Read 1 Peter 2 v 1 - 12.

Revealed mystery *Ephesians 3 v 1 - 7*

It is a pity really that we have to chop Paul's letter into little pieces to study it; we tend to forget that it is a single letter rather than twenty! Still, if we watch out for the 'therefore's and other linking words, with a bit of thought we can piece it together again ...

Read v 1, 14.

Can you work out what Paul is saying? To help us keep his argument in our heads, in v 1 he starts out as if he is going to resume his prayer; but he has something else to add before he actually does! *'For this reason'*: because of God's amazing grace in bringing Gentiles as well as Jews to salvation, Paul prays that they will grasp the glory and wonder of God's love towards them (v 14 - 21). But before he gets on with his prayer he has another dimension to add to our thinking - v 2 - 13. That might take re-reading to digest!

So what is it that Paul adds before going to prayer? *Read v 2 - 7.*

I want you to remember God's amazing grace in trusting me with this message!

The message does not hit us now with anything like the same force. We cannot imagine how stunned both Jew and Gentile would have been when they first heard it. It was totally inconceivable - but gloriously true. It was this (v 6):

> **Gentiles** were to be included in this salvation that sprung from the **Jews**!
> And not only included, but **equal**; joined together in one united body!

Paul calls this message a 'mystery'. Not because it was mind-boggling and totally beyond them to work out. A 'mystery' in the Bible means something ...

... ONCE HIDDEN ... v 5	You thought the Old Testament prophesied of Gentiles being incorporated into God's kingdom? You were right! But nowhere does it speak of this whole new basis of unity and equality. At best the Jews thought of Gentiles becoming 'hangers-on' (though in actual fact they had a blind spot about Gentiles having any part at all in God's kingdom).
... NOW REVEALED v 3, 5	Once it was God's secret, but now He has unwrapped it. First of all it was shown to the apostles and New Testament prophets, and through them to the whole world. It is not to be kept hush-hush, but to be openly declared.
	Read how God first announced it to Peter in Acts 10, 11 (*Read 11 v 4 - 21.*)

Revealed, open - but God's mystery of the gospel has this quality too. It is offensive nonsense to us until God's Spirit (v 5) opens our prejudiced eyes to see it! That is why the Jews so violently persecuted anyone who preached this mystery. And that is why so many who today know the message of the gospel, are strangers to its life-transforming power. Do **you** need to ask God's Spirit to open your eyes to the glory of the gospel ..?

Getting a gospel perspective *Ephesians 3 v 8 - 13*

I'm not sure Paul would have been able to understand us. He was so humbled and amazed by this glorious gospel, he could never get over the privilege of being entrusted with it. He was in love with it! Everything in him burned with passion to tell the world about the unfathomable riches of Christ. How is it then that we can be so indifferent to evangelism? Even when our luke-warm hearts have sluggishly responded to obey our Saviour's commission, how often do we know the awe-filled thrill of the gospel?

Read v 7 - 13.

Pray that you will get hold of Paul's perspective as these verses get hold of you! Because **seeing** right is the key to responding right.

- **He saw himself right (v 8).** This was no false humility - he believed it! It was a standing miracle to the apostle that the person who had the greatest hatred for Jews should be given the greatest privilege. Amazing grace saved him by the gospel - and amazing grace sent him with the gospel! Of course not all are sent to preach, as was the apostle. But all believers are to be ready to tell the gospel.
  Don't you feel so totally unworthy to handle this priceless gospel? *Read 1 Timothy 1 v 11 - 16.*

- **He saw the gospel right (v 8, 10).** *Unsearchable riches of Christ! Manifold wisdom of God!* Have we reduced the gospel to the level of what **man needs**? Begin to explore the infinite treasures of Christ, to gaze on the 'multicoloured' display of the splendour of God's wisdom. First see how glorious God's gospel is - then we will see that it is what man needs!

- **He saw the commission right (v 8, 9).** It was to **preach**! To 'evangelise'! And to make people **see** the truth of the gospel, and how it impacts our lives (the 'fellowship' or 'administration' of the mystery). Yes, people need befriending, bridges need building, but vastly more important than all that is to actually **tell** them - all of them - the Christian gospel.

- **He saw the audience right (v 10).** Not only did Paul long to bring glory to God by making **people** see the gospel; he knew the angels were looking on too. Only through watching the gospel at work in God's people can the angels understand salvation. Whenever a person is saved, a fresh burst of joy resounds through heaven as Christ is praised.
  When did this thought last spur you on to evangelism ...? *Read Luke 15 v 8 - 10.*

But Paul is in prison! Hindered from preaching this gospel as he would like. How frustrating and discouraging! Or was it? *Read v 12, 13 again.*

Like all believers, Paul had intimate access to God Himself through Jesus! Paul might be hindered, but his prayers were not - and the gospel need not be. Never get depressed when you cannot do all you would like to in spreading the gospel. Pray instead!

A mind-blowing prayer — *Ephesians 3 v 14 - 21*

For this reason ..., because of God's grace in calling Gentiles to the same salvation (chapters 1, 2) and because of God's grace in calling Paul to proclaim it (chapter 3), Paul bows to pray that they will know it more and more deeply -

Read v 14 - 21.

How mundane and self-centred so many of our prayers seem when compared with this! He begins by acknowledging a glorious God, carries on with prayer to a glorious God and ends with doxology to a glorious God. Notice how every verse has God right at the centre, while praying for some of the greatest blessings anyone could ever want.

Begins with acknowledging God - v 14 - 16.
It is the **Father** Paul prays to, the Father of Jesus and the whole family of Jews and Gentiles whom He has redeemed. Why, what expectation we should have in coming to a Father who has already given us the greatest of all blessings! And a Father too who has all the 'riches of His glory' at His disposal to hand out to His children!

Carries on with prayer to God - v 16 - 19.
You can't look at one phrase, then leave it behind and go onto the next. All the thoughts tumble into each other like a mountain stream that other streams keep joining as it rushes downwards. The stream gets bigger and grander all the way, reaching a climax in v 19 that leaves us gaping in awed wonder.

With that in mind, what are the great themes of Paul's prayer?
- **Strengthened by the Spirit's indwelling.** Link v 16 with v 17a. The Spirit's power comes to us not so much in fits and starts, but by Christ taking up residence in our hearts. And, though Christ's Spirit already indwells every believer, Paul prays for His powerful presence to become increasingly real as we exercise faith in Him.
- **Know Christ's surpassing love.** Already we are floundering! How can we know infinite love?! Whether we think of the depths of His love that reached us, the breadth of His love stretching out to all His people, or whatever dimension we choose to explore - the more we see the more we realise how much is beyond us.
- **Filled with God's fullness.** To be holy, to be perfect, as He is holy and perfect. To be filled to overflowing with the same perfect characteristics that fill God Himself! Not to become as God, since we are finite and He infinite; but to be so filled with God's likeness as to have no room for anything else.

Ends with doxology to God - v 20, 21.
Can God really give us what Paul is praying? **Will** He do such glorious things for us? Yes, and far more than our highest thoughts can imagine or our strongest faith can expect! Both now, in this life, as we look to Him for them - and ultimately in heaven in their full perfection.

To Him indeed be glory! Bow with Paul in worship.

Instead of any related readings today please spend the time 'praying in' some of the implications of these verses.

Glory through unity *Ephesians 4 v 1 - 6*

'To Him be glory in the church!' That is the high note on which we ended the first half of Ephesians. It was the only appropriate response to all the glorious, mind-stretching teaching we have been treated to.

How meaningful was that response? The true test comes in the practical application of chapters 4 - 6. It is **in the Church** God is glorified; through His people **living** for His glory. Are you still interested ...?

'I ... beseech you,' pleads Paul, *'to walk worthy ...'* (v 1)

Read v 1 - 6.

Not surprisingly his first theme is **UNITY!** How ever could people of such contrasting backgrounds, with such a history of inbred hostility, be joined intimately together in the same church?

BY PUTTING OTHERS FIRST - v 2

Where is 'self' in this verse? Why do we put people down ... or get offended ... or impatient ... or harsh? Why are we too often just the opposite of this verse? Simply because we value ourselves more highly than others; we are the ones who matter most, who are right, who should be noticed! *Read Philippians 2 v 2 - 5.*

For a Jew to have that attitude towards a Gentile was radical to say the least!
Which group, or individuals present the greatest challenge to you?

BY MAKING EVERY ENDEAVOUR - v 3

The task is not as imposible as it may seem; we do not need to **make** unity, only to **keep** it. The unity is already there, as God's Spirit glues believers together with the peace that comes from the cross. Think back to *Ephesians 2 v 14 - 17;* peace though the cross makes peace with one another as well as peace with God.

However, **keeping** that peace is difficult enough. It needs constant, watchful, deliberate, thoughtful effort! For that is the kind of effort Satan is putting in to destroy it ...

BY REMEMBERING WE ARE ONE - v 4 - 6

Think through each of the 7 'one's. How incredibly stupid - and sinful - to let petty grievances drive us apart when we have such massive privileges in common! And not only do we share them - they weld us inseparably together into a single new body.

The same Lord has brought us into the one family of the Father. To belong to the Lord is to belong to one another. To be part of His body, the Church, is to be part of one another. Whether we like it or not, we **are** one. To fail to **express** it is to grieve the Holy Spirit who dwells in each of us. *Read 1 Corinthians 1 v 9 - 13.*

'To Him be glory in the church!' A hollow cry unless we are actively pursuing this unity. There can be little glory where there is little unity ...

Gifts for growth   *Ephesians 4 v 7 - 12*

Unity does not mean uniformity. Christians are not like peas in a pod, but organs of a spiritual body. When believers are treated as if they have rolled off the production line, expected to show the same preferences, to have the same abilities, to be pressed into the same service - then we can never know the **diverse unity** of the New Testament.

God's grace gives believers the same salvation, but **different gifts;** *read v 7 - 12.*

Who gives the gifts? - v 7 - 11

The ascended Christ! Paul uses a vivid quote from Psalm 68, a victory song. It is the Christ who first **descended** to the 'lower parts' - to humble Himself to the earth itself, even to the death of the cross where He took on all the powers of hell.

It is this Christ who has **ascended**; risen victorious over Satan, taking willing captives those who were in his evil captivity. The picture is of Christ leading His people in triumphal march, sharing out His gifts as spoils of the battle.

What are the gifts? - v 11

Many and various - but Paul just mentions a few. Notice how, as always, he gives first place to **teaching** gifts. Although a wide variety of gifts are mentioned in other letters, it is teaching gifts that are basic to the united growth of the Church.

Apostles and prophets were gifts to the early Church, vital to establish the Church's foundation of truth. That foundation has been laid, and recorded for us in the New Testament. We must look for no other revelation of truth.

If the gifts of evangelism, pastoring and teaching are so vital, do you ever ask the acsended Christ for them in your church or others?

What purpose have the gifts? - v 12

For our personal benefit? As a reward for being a good Christian? No! Always for the church! Always to serve the Lord of the church for the growth of His people!

- ❑ **To equip others to serve the Lord** (Best to delete first comma in A.V).
  Ministry is serving - and that does not belong only to the preacher! The work of pastors and teachers is so important **because they lead every believer into ministry in the church!**
- ❑ **To build up the body of Christ.**
  That is hard work for one man to do! But if the whole church is serving the Lord together then it will be a living, growing body, becoming stronger and healthier continually.

If the Lord has given every believer gifts for the growth of His church, are you freely, selflessly using them to serve Him for that purpose?

Read 1 Corinthians 12.

Goals for growth *Ephesians 4 v 13 - 16*

As believers use their gifts to build up the church, what goals do they keep in mind? What are they building to? Verse 13 tells us three things (but first *read v 11 - 16* through a few times to get a feel for the whole section).

- **UNITY (v 13)** Back to the theme of v 1 - 6, but perhaps now we have a broader understanding of it. Unity is not just a lack of disunity! It is living, interactive working together - look at the body picture in *v 16*. The body is co-ordinated, each part helping each other to do what the Head is directing it to - always for the benefit of the whole body.
I cannot imagine a church that has enough unity! Is your church **growing** towards perfect unity?
- **MATURITY (v 13)** ('to a perfect man') Whether we think of the church as a whole, or the individual members of it, the goal is to be 'fully-grown'. That is the whole point of building; not as an exercise in itself, but to reach completion! We are not to stay children, always ready to fall for the latest Christian fad, weak in our understanding of the Bible, never able to distinguish the dangerous from the good. The gales of exciting new ideas sweep many a child off his feet - *v 14*.
- **FULLNESS (v 13)** What is perfect unity and perfect maturity but Christ's own fullness filling His church? To be fully grown is to be full of Christ and empty of self, of ignorance, of weakness. Join with Paul; *'Not that I have already attained, or am already perfected, but I press on ... I press towards the goal ...'* **Read *Philippians 3 v 12 - 16.***

The gifts ... the goals ... then two other ingredients are needed for this work of building up Christ's church. If you like, they are the building materials vital for any progress at all;

TRUTH and LOVE *v 15, 16.*

Never to be sold separately! Truth without love would be too hard, love without truth too soft. The only cement that has any success in building up the church is a smooth blend of the two.

Yes, we must stand for the truth of God's Word. It is a total contradiction to **teach** what the Bible says and **permit** anything and everything that goes on. But is the **way** we stand for the truth likely to win or to alienate? To build up or to pull down?

Yes, we must love one another; we must warmly accept other believers as brothers and sisters in Christ. But true love for Christ and true love for their souls cannot bear to stand by while lives and churches are weakened and ruined by error and sin.

Study Paul's own example! *e.g. Galatians 4 v 16, 19.*

If you are a believer, use your gifts to build up the church in Christ! Use them because you long for full unity, full maturity, Christ's own fullness. And use them wisely, mixing truth with love.

You have not so learned Christ — Ephesians 4 v 17 - 24

A casual observer might conclude that Christians are onto a good thing. For while his own enjoyment of the pleasures of sin is somewhat spoiled by a troublesome conscience and the nagging fear of the consequences, it seems to him as though Christians can freely indulge themselves, knowing that their sins are forgiven, and having a passport to heaven in their back pocket. The onlooker notices that Christians apparently can enjoy any kind of party, get drunk, have sexual relations outside of marriage, listen to any taste of music, watch almost any kind of film, have an unrestricted vocabulary ... yet still be accepted by everyone at church. This thinking onlooker turns away from Christianity in disgust, happy to conclude it is all a sham.

A lot of professing Christians may now be feeling defensive! Is it true for you that at least in some areas you ...
walk as the rest of the Gentiles (heathen, ungodly, unbelievers) *walk* ?

Ask God to help you to be honest in searching your life as you *read v 17 - 20.*

God draws a thick red line between the lives of Christians and non-Christians. The difference in lifestyle is unmistakeable. Their tastes, their pleasures, their standards, their habits, are poles apart. That is, of course, if the 'Christians' are the real thing. Paul knew these Ephesian believers were. When they had heard the gospel it was as if Jesus Himself had spoken to them (v 21). Now Paul could be confident they would respond to his exhortation. They would get rid of clinging heathen habits and live to please their Saviour!

Can you seriously call yourself a Christian yet remain unresponsive to the way Christ wants you to live?

Now read v 20 - 24.

It is time to stop gardening now and go to the wedding. You don't for a moment imagine that your rough mud-splattered clothes will magically transform into spotless suits on the way! Deliberately you take off one set of clothes and replace them by a more appropriate outfit. Similarly a changed life does not happen automatically when you become a Christian. There is some deliberate and drastic getting rid of old ways - and deliberate and radical new habits to form.

Paralleling the two sides of the business emphasises its importance:
 v 22. Put off ... old man ... grows corrupt ... deceitful lusts.
 v 24. Put on ... new man ... created by God ... righteousness and true holiness.

But this is no new teaching of course. Paul is not giving fresh instructions - he is reminding them of what they had been taught 'by Christ' right at the beginning (v 22 follows straight on from v 21). Becoming a Christian is all about a changed life! We are saved not simply from sin's consequences but from sin itself! If you have never 'learned Christ' like this (v 20) then you have never learned Him at all.

Read the similar section in *Colossians; 3 v 1 - 17.*

Overcome evil with good   *Ephesians 4 v 25 - 32*

I remember the day when my chemistry teacher came into the lesson not puffing his pipe. Instead he was sucking extra-strong mints! He had the sense to realise he could never kick his bad habit unless he replaced it with a better one.

Have you learnt that lesson in your Christian life? Holiness does not only mean getting rid of sins - that would lead only to **emptiness**. Christians are to clear all their sins out of their lives by positively, actively **doing good** instead. It is the 'put off ... put on' principle again. Paul sums it up succinctly in Romans 12 v 21;

'Overcome evil with good'

Paul uses that formula as he gets down to five nitty-gritty examples from everyday life. A positive backs up each negative - and both are reinforced with a motivating truth. 'Do not ... instead do ... because'. Try to identify all these elements in each example, as we go through.

Read v 25 - 32.

- **Truth not lying - v 25.** For most young people at least, lying is almost instinctive. Not only isolated lies to avoid trouble, embarrassment or merely inconvenience, but a complex web of cover-up designed to disguise what they really are like. That whole way of thinking must go - and it is not easy. The best way is to practice openness; to deliberately expose yourself to the trust of other believers, so that living a lie becomes impossible. And to talk about the truth together in Bible study will give the best opportunities to open out.
- **Anger not sin - v 26, 27.** Anger and sin nearly always go together. But never with God! If Christians are to be Christ-like they must learn to hate sin with holy, angry hatred. That must replace the restless, festering, resentful anger that leaves us tossing and turning on our beds at night. Then the devil will not be able to get the better of our wrath.
- **Giving not stealing - v 28.** Stealing includes more than fare-dodging, phone-calls on the firm's bill and undeclared casual earnings on the unemployment forms. Any kind of sponging or taking advantage is out. Now we are able to use all our energy and time to maximum advantage, 'as to the Lord', so that we can be on the generous, giving end.
- **Edifying not polluting - v 29, 30.** Is what you say to others like so much bad breath?! Useless and unpleasant? Instead we are to think before speaking; how can we do good by what we say to this person? What will encourage and build them up in the Lord?
  And we must remember that wasted, unsavoury conversation not only harms the people hearing it, but grieves the Holy Spirit who is listening in.
- **Kindness not hostility - v 31, 32.** Thinking ... devising ... speaking ... doing evil. ('clamour' is uncontrolled angry shouting, 'malice' is intention to harm someone) Can you imagine anything less like Jesus? If you have known Jesus' amazing grace in loving you, surely you will fight that evil attitude by actively showing love towards your enemy?

Notice - and take notice of - many similar points in *Romans 12 v 9 - 21.* Remember that last phrase!

No fornicators!   *Ephesians 5 v 1 - 7*

Possibly 5 v 1, 2 belongs better to chapter 4; certainly the two verses fit as part of the antidote to malice! But their theme of Christ's self-giving love is also a suitable introduction to another highly relevant example of putting off the old man and putting on the new;

Read 4 v 31 - 5 v 7. We will start with the **exhortation** itself, then look at the **motivation** that comes before and after.

SERIOUS EXHORTATION - v 3, 4

'Can you imagine anything less like Jesus?' I wrote of 4 v 31. This is just as true of 5 v 3, 4! Of all the examples, Paul singles out this one as 'not fitting' for Christians. There is nothing more out of place for a 'saint' than to be immersed in moral filth, nothing more alien to a Christian than all the coarse jokes and smutty inuendos that go along with loose living.

- *'let it not even be named among you'* We are to be so separate from any kind of immoral behaviour that there is never to be even a hint of it among Christians. Flirting, compromising situations, covetous eyes will no longer be a cause for anxiety for fellow believers; films, programmes, books, newspapers with any unhealthy sex-element will be foreign to us; suggestive remarks, dubious humour, loose vocabulary will never be overheard! We have fallen so far from this standard; the challenge is to reject popular opinion and live how **God** tells us to!
- *'but rather giving of thanks'* That is the Christian replacement for immorality! Giving thanks for our bodies, giving thanks that they belong to God, giving thanks for husband or wife. God is no kill-joy, robbing us of the best pleasures! Rather He shows us how to guard the most special and intimate gifts against perversion and pollution. There is so much to thank God for in marriage, but you never can thank Him for any kind of sexual relationship or even exploration outside of marriage.

STIRRING MOTIVATION - v 1, 2, 5 - 7

Most Christians know what is right - and want to do it. But the pressures, the examples, the temptation, the excitement get the better of them. 'Just a little' indulging leads quickly to outright immorality. Paul knows we need the strongest motivation to help us live right - and that is what he gives:

- *'dear children'* (v 1). How can we return the tender love of our heavenly Father with filthy rebellion! If we love God we will certainly want to be followers of God - to be like Him and obedient to Him.
- *'given Himself for us'* (v 2). In the face of the cross can we not give up the 'me'? Instead of offering ourselves up to our own sinful passions, to give ourselves fully up to Him? *Romans 6 v 19 - 23.*
- *'no fornicator ... has any inheritance'* (v 5). All the while you indulge in such sin you can have no hope of heaven. That passport you have does not have God's stamp on it; it will not get you in. *Revelation 22 v 14, 15.*
- *'wrath of God ... sons of disobedience'* (v 6) After all you will prove not to be one of His 'dear children' if you persist in disobedience. Along with the rest of disobedient mankind you must face His wrath not His love. *Revelation 21 v 7, 8.*

Therefore... '(v 7). Surely, with all that powerful motivation you will respond and return to a grieved but forgiving Saviour ...?

Children of light   *Ephesians 5 v 8 - 14*

What God has done for His dear children ... what God will do to the disobedient ... Now a further motivation to live as we should - *How God has changed us who believe.*

Read v 8 - 14.

Once darkness ... now light!

Not only were we **in** the dark, ignorantly pursuing our sinful desires - we were actually part and parcel of that darkness. We were darkness itself ... but now we are light itself! Whereas before we contributed to the world's depravity, now we are shining out light and truth.

If we belong to Jesus the light of the world we **are** lights - but the question is whether we actively **shine out** like Him; *read v 8 and Matthew 5 v 14 - 16.*

If we really are children of light, argues Paul, then surely we will ...

- **Bear fruit - v 9, 11.**
  Try growing tomatoes in a blacked out shed and see what crop you get! Benefits reaped from a life of darkness are nil; nothing of lasting good for yourself or anyone else. But now it is different ... is it? **Goodness** has replaced malice, **righteousness** has ousted crookedness, **truth** is there instead of falseness. *Read Galatians 5 v 19 - 25.*

- **Discover what pleases the Lord - v 10.**
  Before we only proved what was unacceptable to God - at least when our consciences were working. But now is there that joy and peace telling us that God loves it when we live by His Word? *(Romans 12 v 1, 2)*

- **Have nothing to do with darkness - v 11, 12.**
  It is nonsense to imagine we can be purely positive in our Christian witness. There is an awful lot of darkness around that needs rejecting point blank. 'No fellowship' means that, contrary to popular opinion, darkness is never to be won by joining in with it. In fact there are many things that are so abhorrent to us that we just have to leave the group when they become the talking point ... do we?

- **Expose the darkness - v 11, 13.**
  Not by keeping ourselves to ourselves; they will simply think we are unfriendly. No, the light must shine **in the darkness**, not just where it is already light! Never be embarrassed at not wanting to join in with their darkness; rather expose it by showing how much richer and more fruitful and better in every way your Christian life is. But is it ...?

Does your life match up to this description of children of light? Whether you have backslidden, or never known this truly Christian life, let Paul's exhortation sink in -

read v 14.

Be wise, be filled! *Ephesians 5 v 15 - 21*

It's not that there are glaring inconsistencies in your Christian life ... you are not indulging in the 'darkness' of the world ... indeed you are concerned to be a witness to Christ ... **but there has been so little fruit, so little growth, so little usefulness.**

Granted, we are not always the best judges of ourselves - nevertheless do the next few verses shed any light? *Read v 15 - 17.*

Jonathan Edward's 70th (!) resolution reads *'Resolved: Never to lose one moment of time, but to improve it in the most profitable way I possibly can.'*

That was wisdom. Sinners abuse their time, fools lose their time, wise people use their time. And they use it **wisely**. Understanding the Lord's will (v 17), they get their priorities right, not using up large chunks of time on unimportant tasks or pastimes. Recognising that the days are evil (v 16) and knowing how few are living for the Lord, they seize every opportunity to do good.

'Do not be unwise ...' It is not intended as an option for the energic, but a command for all God's people ... *Read Psalm 90 v 12.*

True wisdom is **Spirit-filled** wisdom. We obey v 17 by obeying v 18; *read v 18 - 21.*
Do not be drunk with wine! ... be filled with the Spirit!

There can be few things so unwise as emptying our senses with alcohol. The way to live a full, rich, fruitful life is for God's Spirit to be continually filling us. While it is He who does the filling, it is we who are exhorted to see to it that we are filled! Paul gives us four ways to prepare ourselves for the Spirit's filling:

- ❏ *speaking together in song* (v 19). How encouraging it can be to sing together! We may find it hard to express just how we feel, but a song or a psalm or hymn can put it perfectly.
- ❏ *singing praise to the Lord* (v 19) We sing not only to benefit one another, but to exalt the Lord together. Notice, the melody that counts is made **in the heart** - is yours good at singing?
- ❏ *giving thanks always for all things* (v 20). That is, all the Father has given us; knowing that how ever it seems to us at the time, He only gives **good** gifts.
- ❏ *submitting to one another* (v 21). Does that somehow seem out of place, different from the other three? No, because God is interested in the whole body of the church worshipping Him **together**, not independently! Will His Spirit fill us while we are self-centred, superior, insensitive to other believers?

Be filled with the Spirit! Not by sitting, empty-minded, waiting for an ecstatic experience. That is something other than the Spirit's work. No, by giving our minds and hearts to sing songs of praise and encouragement together, with continual gratitude to the Lord and humble respect for one another.

This is the way to learn to be wise - and how to live out Jonathan Edward's resolution. Like Barnabas; *Acts 11 v 22 - 24.*

As Christ and His Church   *Ephesians 5 v 22 - 33*

In a climate of cheap, sex-centred love and fragile, throwaway relationships, it is vital to keep saturating ourselves with God's own principles for marriage. Right from the beginning of our first clumsy efforts to find a partner we need to keep asking what God's views are on relationships. The answers from this section are simply staggering. We will not easily play around with the opposite sex if we even begin to see the lofty, sacred heights to which God elevates marriage.

Read v 22 - 33.

Wives submit! 'Lofty heights'? you ask. Yes, when we see how God highly values the humble. Yes, when we see it as a picture of full adoring surrender to our Lord and Master. Yes, when we see it as an ultimate expression of self-giving love to the man who cares and leads, protects and provides, listens and loves. Yes, because God sees a humble, submissive spirit as 'very precious'. *Read 1 Peter 3 v 1 - 6.*

Submit as believers submit to their Head; fully, unconditionally, willingly, in everything (v 24). Submit not because he is anything other than your equal, but because God has given him responsibility to be the head. Submit not to his better judgement, his greater ability, his dominant character - the woman may be superior in all these ways - but to the position **God** has given him.

Read 1 Corinthians 11 v 3, then *Ephesians 5 v 22 - 24 again.*

Husbands love! There are no doubts about 'lofty heights' here! If women find their commission hard then the men's task is impossible! How can our poor, faltering, self-polluted love even begin to resemble the infinite, unchangeable, self-giving love of a crucified Saviour? In a sense of course it cannot - yet in another way it must, if husbands are to obey this very real command. How?

- **By giving himself (v 25).** Love is not feeling excited, it is not **receiving** nice sensations. It is **giving out**, it is spending ourselves, it is sacrificing comfort, money, time, pleasure for someone else, it is selfless and costly, active and practical. Think of the cross if you want to understand love.
- **By having a purpose (v 26, 27).** Christ's love had a goal - not for Himself, but for His bride! He was determined to make her pure and holy, perfect in every way. A husband's love will want the very best for his wife; not to spoil and pamper her with endless luxuries, but to help and encourage her to holiness and heaven.
- **By counting her as himself (v 28 - 32).** It is not selfish to care for himself; it is instinctive and natural. But it is to be equally as instinctive and natural to respond to his wife's needs; for she is part of him. Just as Christ, astonishingly, counts His people as His own flesh and bones, so husband and wife are inseparably welded in intimate union.

Wives submit! Husbands love! Ultimately these are two distinctive ways of expressing the same attitude; **self-giving, Christ-like, devotion to one another.** That is the only possible basis for true relationship.

Radical principles   *Ephesians 6 v 1 - 9*

If our Christianity does not reach home it cannot be worth much. Paul is just as concerned about a peaceful united family as he is about a peaceful united church.

CHILDREN and PARENTS - *read v 1 - 4.*

Rebellion is in our bones. None of us naturally like to be told what to do - and don't if we can avoid it. But Paul gives four strong reasons for children to obey their parents:

- **It is right (v 1).** Instinctively we know it is. Even when society tells us we do not have to listen to anyone, children world over know it is right to obey their parents.
- **It is commanded (v 2).** Disobeying parents is rebellion against God.
- **It is good for us (v 3).** Contrary to what we believe at the time, it is better for us - God has promised! The happiest children are obedient children.
- **It is Christian (v 1).** 'In the Lord'; out of love for Christ believers surely will obey ...

The four strong reasons apply even for the worst parents. But how much more reason gladly to obey when we have parents who live by v 4! Praise God if you have tender - but firm - parents who train and teach and encourage you to follow the Lord. And although you will not be bound to **obey** them after becoming independent, you will always be reluctant to **grieve** them.

Compare with *Colossians 3 v 20, 21.* What further points come out?

SERVANTS and MASTERS *read v 6 - 9.*

Obviously our situation is very different; but the principles apply equally well to modern employment. Four challenging labour reforms - all springing from knowing it is **Christ** we are serving first and foremost.

- **with fear and trembling (v 5).** Not quivering with fright at the sound of Boss' footsteps, but a fear of dishonouring the Lord by carelessness, laziness or insensitivity.
- **In sincerity of heart (v 5).** Singlemindedly, wholeheartedly - and without ulterior motives.
- **regardless of who is watching (v 6).** It makes no difference because it is the Lord you are serving - and He is always watching.
- **With good will (v 7)** Cheerful and willing to go the extra mile; even when it means unpaid overtime ...

Pay is not the issue anyway; since it is the Lord we are serving it is His reward we can expect. And we can surely trust Him to treat His servants generously? (v 8).

But that is no excuse for stingy bosses! The golden rule applies to them; bosses must 'do the same things to them'. If they want respect they must show it; if they want a pay rise then they should think about giving one. They too are to serve a far higher Master; and the One who rewards not status or success, but service to Him.

Is it really **Christ** you are serving? It is important not to rush off without letting these radical principles sink in. What practical difference will each make to your work or study?

Read Colossians 3 v 22 - 4 v 1 to identify the same principles. Any new ones?

| The Opposition | Ephesians 6 v 10 - 13 |

'It's easy - just go away and put them into practice!' That is definitely not Paul's closing message for us! He has given believers high, challenging ideals to live by; now we have been shown how to live in unity in Christ, whatever the barriers that once divided, to value one another's gifts as we work together, to put off all the clinging characteristics of the old man, overcoming evil by pursuing holiness, to expose the darkness by living as light, to be filled with the Spirit, to have harmonious self-giving relationships at home and work!

But anyone who thinks it will be easy is going to be disillusioned in five minutes flat. However determined you are to reform, there is someone who is more determined to stop you. And he is far stronger, far cleverer and far more devious than you;

Read v 10 - 13.

Like it or not, for a Christian the fight is on. Opting out means defeat - and that is no option if you truly are on the Lord's side. Opting in leads to victory; but we need to grasp a couple of basic rules of encounter:

Know your enemy!

People love to mythologise the devil. Gruesome fire-breathing ogres with evil grins reassure the world that it is all harmless fantasy. The devil loves it too; he can get a lot more done if he is unobserved and unopposed. *Know your enemy* first of all by reckoning with him as a reality! He is there all right, manoevering his hosts of evil spirits and powers (v 12) to do maximum harm. Not that we are to fall into the opposite trap (his own of course) of imagining devils hiding behind every spiritual lamppost, so we begin to blame our every failure and sin on Satan. Then *know your enemy* too by knowing what he is like. He is not like some schoolboy bully, out for a bit of malicious fun. He is out to destroy, to pull us into hell. And a particular feature is his devious, unethical stratagems (v 11). He will stop at no tactic, twisting and deceiving to the best advantage, attacking when we are at our weakest, even using other Christians, if he can, to catch us off guard.

Fight your enemy!

Fairly obvious really, yet many Christians seem to imagine he will go away if they ignore him, or that God will sort him out. But Paul, therefore God, is insistent. It is we Christians who are to **be strong** to **put on** armour, to **stand**, to **wrestle**. We are to run from sin but never from the devil; we are to stand and fight and not stop until it is he who runs.   *Read 1 Peter 5 v 8, 9.*

Fight, but never single handedly and never unarmed. Again so obvious if we remember the kind of enemy we have; and yet we seem constantly to make the mistake! It is **in the Lord** we are to be strong, **His might** we must rely on, **His armour** that we are to put on, so we can stand prepared to face Satan's attacks. *Read the section* once more.

It might be hard, but Paul is certainly not discouraging us from living out the last couple of chapters. Far from it! Go and put them into practice - but be ready for a fight. Every day put God's armour on and stride into battle depending on the strength of the conquering Lord.   *Read 1 Timothy 6 v 11 - 16.*

The Armour *Ephesians 6 v 14 - 17*

Whose armour? God's. Keep that firmly in mind and it will help us to interpret this vivid imagery of a fully-equipped Roman soldier. Every item is fully devil-proof because it centres on what God has perfectly done. And yet it is useless to us unless we put it on, and unless we put **each** piece on (v 13);

Read v 14 - 17.

BELT *truth*	The soldier's tunic was tucked up into his belt to stop him tripping up in battle. Satan will do his worst to trip us up with false teaching. Test everything you hear with this question: *Is it God's truth? Is it what the Bible teaches?*
BREASTPLATE *righteousness*	If the devil fails to trip you up perhaps he will go straight for the heart. How will you counter his accusations of sin and failure? *When Satan tempts me to despair. And tells me of the guilt within Upward I look and see Him there, Who made an end of all my sin.* Jesus' righteousness is mine, Satan! It covers all my sin and failure.
BOOTS *gospel*	Sore feet make us reluctant to move far! But Roman soldiers had designer-boots, to cover large distances with amazing speed and then still feel ready for battle! Gospel boots are what we need to keep on! Instead of focusing on our own problems and needs, to be looking to Jesus, rejoicing in His peace through the cross. That is the way to stay fresh and ready for battle.
SHIELD *faith*	A shield is not put on, but held up to intercept the flaming arrows aimed at you. Faith must be used to be any good. Satan's lethal darts of temptation to sin, of pain, of trouble, of dashed hopes, can only be safely extinguished by putting trust in Christ. Combat Satan's seducing lies by clinging onto God's promises and God's character.
HELMET *salvation*	With all these missiles flying about there is only one way to hold up our heads with confidence and face the battle. We need the helmet on! We need to know that Christ has saved us! We cannot fight if we are hesitant and doubting as to whose side we are on. We must put our full confidence in Christ's promises to save.
SWORD *Word*	Well-protected now, but a soldier does not simply stand in the middle of the battlefield waiting for the enemy to run out of ammunition. He is on the attack. One weapon is enough to see off all opposition if it used right. God's Word driven home by God's Spirit cannot be resisted. Know your Bible inside out! Pray that God will make you a skilful soldier in knowing just how to use it.

What lessons do we learn from Jesus' way of dealing with Satan's attacks? *Luke 4 v 1 - 13; Mark 8 v 31 - 33.*

The prayer   *Ephesians 6 v 18 - 24*

The armour has been described, but before hastily trying to pull it on, there is a secret to learn. **God's armour will not go on without prayer!**

Read v 18 - 20.

There is nothing casual or routine about the prayer that is required. God's army is no place for sloppy, half-hearted, occasional prayer. Take to heart the four 'alls' (v 18).

- **ALWAYS:** Continually, without slackening. On all occasions, in every situation. Prayer is to saturate our living.
- **ALL PRAYER AND SUPPLICATION:** Not a few set phrases! There is tremendous breadth and variety called for - and don't forget the supplications, the specific requests that are like arrows aimed at particular enemy targets.
- **ALL PERSEVERANCE:** Never give up watching for the answers! Never give up praying when the answers don't come!
- **ALL SAINTS:** Go it alone at your peril! The Church of God is to move forward as a mighty army, not as a few isolated heroes. Pray for the weak! Pray for the uninvolved ones! Pray for the backsliders!

Watch and pray! is Jesus' urgent call to His soldiers facing battle. Instead the disciples slept... *Read Matthew 26 v 36 - 56.*

'And for me!' pleads Paul. Because the battle is not largely to do with the church **surviving** but **conquering.** The gospel is to spread, the enemy front is to be pushed back. So pray for gospel preachers, pray for missionaries and evangelists. And pray specifically for ...

- **UTTERANCE (v 19).** Literally 'word'. The preacher must not depend on his own ability or oratory; pray for the Holy Spirit to give the right words so the message goes home clearly and powerfully.
- **BOLDNESS (v 19, 20).** If the gospel loses its offence it loses its power. Paul knew how he 'ought to speak' but even he needed God's courage to do it. Don't take a preacher's boldness for granted - pray for it.

Paul knew he had the love and prayers of the believers in Asia Minor; yet they needed information to fuel their prayers. Tychicus was a trusted messenger; he would tell them the latest about Paul's situation at Rome and particular opportunities.

Read v 21 - 24.

The convention in letter writing then was to send 'wishes'. But Paul's wishes are prayers (v23, 24); prayers for the deepest blessings God can give, for the believers he dearly loves. What greater things can we ask for those we genuinely care about? ...

'Peace ... love ... grace be with all those who love our Lord Jesus Christ in sincerity!'

OUTLINE: Ephesians - Christ and His body

🔑 *... that He might reconcile them both (Jew and Gentile) to God in one body through the cross.* (2 v 16)

☞ Sum up each section in a short sentence or phrase (ideas below).
☞ Look for key words in each section (usually repeated).

SECTION	SUMMARY	KEYWORDS
1 v 1- 14		
v 15- 23		
2 v 1 - 10		
v 11 - 18		
v 19 - 22		
3 v 1 - 13		
v 14 - 21		
4 v 1 - 6		
v 7 - 16		
v 17 - 24		
v 25 - 32		
5 v 1 - 7		
v 8 - 14		
v 15 - 21		
v 22 - 33		
6 v 1 - 9		
v 10 - 20		
v 21 - 24		

children, parents. servants, masters ... spiritual blessings in Christ ... closing greetings ... God's building ... that you may be filled! ... As one, be one ... be wise! be filled! ... no uncleanness ... overcoming evil with good ... that you may know! ... saved by grace ... New man ... marriage - Christ and the church ... the whole armour of God ... gifts for growth ... children of light ... mystery revealed, mystery preached ... the two made one in Christ

FACT - FILE : Philippians

PHILIPPIANS

Christ-minded

THE CHURCH

- Philippi was Paul's first stop in Europe, on his second missionary journey. An important Greek city with the privileged status of a Roman colony. See map on page 158.
- Acts 16 records the first two converts, Lydia and the jailor; the nucleus out of which the Philippian church sprung.
- The Philippian church was a great source of joy to Paul, taking an active interest in the spread of the gospel and supporting him financially.
- Danger was threatening the church, however, both from outside opposition and false teaching, and from internal divisions.

THE LETTER

- Probably written during Paul's first imprisonment at Rome (AD 61 - 63), around ten years after the founding of the church at Philippi.
- Epaphroditus had brought a gift from the Philippian church to Paul in prison. Paul sends back his reply with Epaphroditus; a warm-hearted response to their concern for him.
- It is hard to identify a single purpose for writing; though Paul is clearly picking up on concerns which Epaphroditus would have shared with him.
  - He encourages them in their involvement in the spread of the gospel.
  - He urges them to stand fast, despite the pressures and opposition.
  - He exhorts them to be united, taking on the humble mind of Christ.
  - He tells them to follow his example of single-minded determination to gain Christ and rejoice in Him alone.
  - He rejoices in their giving.

  Although there are some strongly-worded warnings, the whole tone is upbeat - full of joy and full of Christ.
- There is no simple structure, and little theological argument. Encouragement, exhortation and example are interweaving strands.

If at all possible ...

Find time to read the letter through in one sitting, with this background in mind.

'I thank my God...'   *Philippians 1 v 1 - 6*

Many of us are probably guilty of scribbling boring thankyou letters in a half-hearted, dutiful way. Paul's 'thankyou' letter to the Philippians is just the opposite - crammed with purpose and bursting with life, as he shows his gratitude and love to the generous believers at Philippi.

Read v 1 - 6.

Typically, Paul does not start his letter by thanking the Philippians for their gift, but by thanking his God for the Philippians!

Who were these Philippian believers? We know about two of them - *read Acts 16 v 12 - 15, 25 - 34.* Especially notice verses 15 and 34. Right from the beginning of their Christian life, these believers showed their love to God - and His messenger Paul - in very practical ways.

Two gems that Paul must have highly prized! But we must guard against forming an idealised picture of New Testament churches. They were all made up of human beings, saved sinners, with all the variety of problems and weaknesses that we are too familiar with. Nevertheless, this church at Phillipi gave special joy to the apostle ...

❑ **WHEN DOES HE GIVE THANKS FOR THEM?** (v 3)
Thinking of the Philippians was like a tonic to Paul! It always had the same effect, of lifting his heart in praise to God.
Are there many you could say the same for? If not, is that their fault or yours?
Are there many who could say the same about you? If not, why not?

❑ **WHAT DOES HE GIVE THANKS FOR?** (v 5, 6)
Notice the two main things. (No mention of their generous giving yet!)
Why do these mean so much to him?
Do you often thank God for these same things?

❑ **WHO DOES HE GIVE THANKS TO?** (v 3)
Even unbelievers talk of 'feeling thankful'. But that is a strange expression really; who is their thanks directed towards? Believers have no need to be vague; let us unashamedly talk of 'thanking **my God**'!
Paul knew who to thank. He had not forgotten who it was that had transformed these men and women and given them such loving, generous hearts. God had done it all, and God would do all there was left to do (v 6) - to God be all the praise!

It is obviously good to pray for other believers, sometimes with pain and heartache for the time of trouble or backsliding they are going through. But how many of our requests are 'with joy'? (v 4) If you have neglected thanking your God for all He has done for others, ask for forgiveness for that ingratitude, and grace to thank Him with genuine joy.

Praying for friends ***Philippians 1 v 7 - 11***

Often a friendship will start because we have something in common with another person. That was certainly true for Paul and the Philippian believers. And the friendship was very special, because what they shared was so special. Something they all loved and worked for - and were even prepared to suffer for.

PAUL AND THE PHILIPPIANS	❑ LOVED ❑ WORKED TO SPREAD	➤	THE GOSPEL

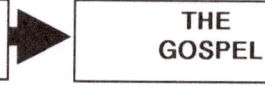

THE GOSPEL explained Paul's deep love for them (v 8). It was for the gospel they had shown such concern for Paul in prison. It was the gospel's progress in the world they were so interested in, both in **defending** it against false teaching and **confirming** it, proclaiming it positively (v 7). And that made Paul just burn with love for them!

THE GOSPEL explained Paul's deep confidence in them (v 7)! Because they shared his love for the gospel he was convinced they shared in the same grace of salvation.

What does 'fellowship in the gospel' really mean (v 5)? Many Christians complain of lacking fellowship, but is the real problem that they lack a meaningful participation in the spread of the gospel?

Paul was shut away in prison 800 miles away from these Philippian believers, but he was not complaining of a lack of fellowship with them!

Paul certainly values the love of the Philippian believers - but he is not satisfied! He prays that their love and knowledge of Christ will keep growing.

Read his prayer - *verses 9 - 11.*

> ❑ Identify at least four main longings.
> ❑ Think about why Paul chose these - he really **meant** them; they are not simply nice-sounding words!
> ❑ Are these the things you want for yourself?
> ❑ Are these the things you ask God to give your **friends**, or are your prayers for them restricted to everyday concerns (job, health etc.)?

Compare with another great prayer of Paul's; *Ephesians 3 v 14 - 21.*

❑ Think why our prayers are often so pigmy-sized in comparison.
❑ How can we develop the same burning concerns as Paul? (e.g *time spent with God ... getting priorities right...*)

Good news   Philippians 1 v 12 - 18

It had been a long wait for the Philippian believers. What was the news from Rome - how was the gospel progressing? It had taken months for their messenger to do the round trip, having been taken seriously ill on route (2 v 27). But at last he was back (having successfully delivered their gift to Paul) bearing reassuring news ...

Read v 12 - 18.

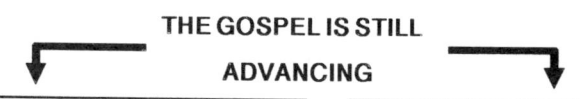

THE GOSPEL IS STILL ADVANCING

verses 12, 13 — BY PAUL'S WITNESS

You can imagine the Philippian believers' distress and frustration over the great apostle being shut away in prison - when he could have been preaching the gospel to hundreds!

But Paul is not thinking like that. He wants them to praise God for the remarkable opportunities he had as a prisoner - to those who otherwise may not have heard the gospel.

Who? (see also chapter 4 v 22!)

The God who turned everything in Paul's life into advantage for the gospel will do the same in our lives. Let's expect gospel opportunities - and take them!

verses 14 - 17 — BY OTHER PREACHERS

It seems amazing, but they had actually been encouraged to speak **more** bravely by Paul's imprisonment! How God can turn round situations just as He pleases to fulfil His own purposes!

Not all the preachers had pure motives, but still **the truth** was preached - that was the important thing to Paul.

Are we as thrilled by the spread of the gospel truth - **even by those we don't altogether agree with?**

'CHRIST IS PREACHED!'

That alone is enough to make Paul rejoice. In fact he seems determined not to let his circumstances get him down and blur his vision (v 18). He will keep joy alive by focussing not on himself but on the spread of the gospel.

It is easy to find reasons to be discouraged about the work of the gospel! As an antidote let's pay more attention to rejoicing over the way Christ is being clearly preached all over the world.

'Christ is preached ... I ... will rejoice.' *Read Isaiah 52 v 7 - 10.*

A matter of life or death *Philippians 1 v 19 - 26*

So the gospel was being preached, but what about their great friend, Paul? How was he? Paul was concerned that the Philippians should not be worried about him. It is true that his trial was due to take place shortly; but whatever the outcome, Paul was sure it would be the best one; *read v 19, 20.*

Whether RELEASE or DEATH, Paul knew it would work out for ...
- his salvation (v 19) - in other words, it was all part of the 'good work' in his life that God was bringing to the ultimate goal of being with Him for ever (v 6).
- Christ being exalted or magnified in him (v 20).

So why worry? Paul knew he could safely trust God to secure the best future for him.

Now Paul weighs up the two possibilities in his mind - *read v 19 - 26.*

DEATH	LIFE
'GAIN' (v 21)	'IS CHRIST' (v 21)
'DESIRE TO DEPART' (v 23)	'FRUIT' (v 22)
'TO BE WITH CHRIST' (v 23)	'MORE NEEDFUL FOR YOU' (v 24)
'FAR BETTER' (v 23)	'FOR YOUR ... FURTHERANCE (PROGESS) AND JOY' (v 25)

Obviously your situation will be different from Paul's, but it would be useful to do a similar balancing exercise. Would you prefer life or death? Think through the two lists again, comparing your attitudes to life and to death with Paul's.

Read 2 Corinthians 5 v 1 - 10.

A young Turkish believer, Kenan Araz, lay waiting for the serious operation which offered only a slim chance of saving his life. Suddenly he burst into song, praising God. The reason? *'I'm so happy. You see, the thing is, I **know** that if I die tonight I'm going to live with Jesus Christ forever. And if I live - well I'll live for Him.'*

'For to me to live is Christ, and to die is gain' (v21)

But the real thrust of these verses is that Paul was not thinking first about himself! It was the life-or-death of the churches at Philippi and elsewhere that was occupying his thinking. They needed encouraging, they needed teaching and building up! Never mind his own joy over going to be with Christ - what joy it would bring them if he stayed! Yes, if the choice were his, Paul had no doubt what it would be.

Read v 24 - 26 again.

Have you ever considered putting your own spiritual needs after the needs of others in the church? In what practical ways might that apply? How can we increase the joy of others?

Suffering for the gospel Philippians 1 v 27 - 30

Why has Paul spent so long spelling out his own attitudes to his danger and suffering in prison?

Because all Christians are going to suffer, when the gospel is their priority! And the church at Philippi was no exception. Paul was anxious they should continue to stand firm like he had, united in their determination to face the opposition.

Read 27 - 30 and compare with *v 18 - 20.*

Philippi was no easy situation in which to spread the gospel. Paul and Silas had discovered that early on, when they were thrown into prison for their pains (Acts 16). There was certainly the constant opposition of a heathen idol-worshipping, immoral city - but there were also more specific 'adversaries' (v 28) who seemed bent on attacking the gospel work in Philippi (See chapter 3 v 2, 18, 19 - apparently a mixture of those teaching circumcision and others recommending licentious, immoral behaviour.)

So what is Paul's advice to us when gospel work gets tough? Bury your head in the sand? Keep a low profile until the opposition goes away? He tells us to ...

- **Stand together!** *v 27.*
    They are to present a solid battle-front,
        - standing together **against** the opposition.
        - striving together **for** the gospel truth.
    And the only way we will do that is to **live** by the gospel we are fighting for! Disunity will break up the ranks as soon as our behaviour towards one another loses touch with the gospel.

- **Do not be frightened of the opposition!** *v 28, 29.*
    Persecution cannot harm you! For the persecutors it certainly is serious, but for the persecuted it only spells salvation (remember v 19). The worst they can do to you turns out to be a gift from God (v 28b, 29)! He not only gives faith to believe in Christ but suffering to prove and strengthen that faith.
    Read Jesus' early instructions to the twelve disciples - *Matthew 10 v 16 - 39.*

Read v 30.

Are you sharing the same conflicts as Paul and the Philippians?

Don't give up on striving together with others for the gospel! · Don't return God's gift of suffering for Christ's sake ...

Like Christ Philippians 2 v 1 - 4

The Philippian church was being threatened...
- By a hostile society;
- In a less obvious way, **from within the church itself.**

Read chapter 1 v 27 and 2 v 1 - 4.

What kind of attitudes is Paul warning against? What sort of behaviour do you think was threatening the church at Philippi? (And has torn apart many churches of true believers ever since.)

- Pick out all the phrases in the reading which describe the **wrong** attitudes.
- Pick out all the phrases that tell us the **right** kind of attitude.

It is worth reading them several times. Pray them through to take them to heart. Try to think of real live situations, and practical ways of showing this humble, uniting spirit which values others above yourself.

You may have been hardly moved by what Paul is saying here, and left feeling rather cold -

Read v 1, 2 again.

Now can you see some good reasons for taking notice of Paul's teaching? What have you known of Christ's compassion, His comfort, His love, His friendship, His tenderness, His mercy?

Paul's reasoning has tremendous force;

Since you have known this, surely you will show Christ's attitudes towards others.

Have we known? ... So will we show...?

Read Ephesians 4 v 31 - 5 v 2.

Jesus' mind, Jesus' glory   *Philippians 2 v 5 - 11*

If Paul has failed to shift our proud, self-seeking behaviour by his appeals in v 1 - 4, then surely no believer will remain unresponsive to the supreme example of humility?

Read v 2 - 4 with Jesus in mind, then *v 5 - 8.*

ALTHOUGH HE ...
- is fully God, enjoying absolute equality with the Father in the glory of heaven,

NEVERTHELESS HE ...
- emptied Himself of all the honour that belonged to Him.
- came to serve sinful mankind, not to be waited upon.
- took on the limitations of a real human man.
- humbled Himself to the point of dying for the sins of others; bearing even the curse of crucifixion for the sake of His people.

Follow the points through the verses, then link them to *Isaiah 53 v 2 - 6.*

Spend a while praising the Lord for His awesome self-sacrifice in coming to save sinners like us from our rebellion against Him.

But don't miss the whole point: for believers **HE IS OUR EXAMPLE!**

Read v 5 again. Consider how much honour you deserve - and how far you are prepared to go in giving up your own interests to *'look out ... for the interests of others'* (v 4)

Paul follows great challenge with great encouragement. What will God do for the one who humbles himself like his Saviour? -

Read v 9 - 11.

The lowest conceivable humility - the highest conceivable glory!

If you have praised Jesus for what He went through for you, then you will be joyfully echoing these verses! Yes, Jesus alone is worthy! Jesus deserves the acclamation of the universe that He is Lord. *Revelation 5 v 12 - 14* expresses the believer's feelings.

One day we will be there with Him, exalted by God - if now we will humble ourselves like Him ...

Shining lights　　　　　　　　　　　　　　　　　*Philippians 2 v 12 - 18*

What a Saviour! So majestic and glorious. And yet the awesome Example of deep humility. What should be our response to this? How should believers live out the Christian life (*'work out your salvation'* v 12)?

Read v 12 - 14.
- *'Fear and trembling'* (v 12)
  Fear of offending the Saviour. Fear of hurting His people and damaging His church.
- Remembering *'it is God who works in you'* (v 13)
  We only work at Christlikeness because God is already at work in us! It is **His** purpose to bring our salvation to completion. **His** pleasure is at issue. That is reassuring when we seem to fail so much!
- *'without murmuring or disputing'* (v 14)
  Complaining? Quarrelling? That is not God working in us! That is not Christlike humility!

These are Paul's intended results from considering Jesus' example. Our love and gratitude for His death on the cross needs to be measured by the degree of Christlike humility it produces ...

Christlikeness **inside** the church is the key to Christlikeness in the world **outside** -

Read v 15, 16.

The city of Philippi was in great darkness.
- How does Paul describe its inhabitants? Does it fit your town / work environment?
- What must the believers at Philippi be like? Think of each description in turn.

What a contrast! They are to shine like stars in the darkness. As God's children, they are to be a living testimony to the truth of God's Word which they are to show to everyone around (verse 16).

And remember the qualification for believers to shine as lights in the darkness - CHRISTLIKENESS! How can I expect to be a good witness to people around if I am a critical, proud, selfish member of my church!?

Read 1 Peter 2 v 9 - 12.

Now read Philippians 2 v 16 - 18.

Paul could wish for no more. If only the church at Philippi would be HUMBLE and SHINING, like Christ, then he would count all his labour for them a tremendous joy. He had his sights fixed on Christ's coming again when he would see just how worthwhile it was to pour out his life as an offering for these believers.

Who better than Timothy?   *Philippians 2 v 19 - 24*

Verses 1 - 4 are still Paul's theme! If Jesus' supreme example seems so far beyond us, then what about quiet, unassuming Timothy?

Read v 19 - 24, comparing with *v 1 - 4.*

What kind of character had Paul chosen to send to the Philippian church?

- **Genuine carer** (v 20). There was no-one like Timothy with such a heart for people. There are plenty of gifted, committed Sunday School teachers who will do a reasonable job, but those who will **never stop caring** for the children are like gold!

- **Christ-pleaser** (v 21). That is the explanation of v 20. Timothy had a heart for people because he had a heart for Christ.
  We can spend all day meditating on Christ, but if we have little concern for Christ's gospel in Christ's church, then in Paul's books we are those who *'seek their own, not the things of Christ'...*

- **Proven servant.** (v 22). Paul was taking no risks in sending Timothy. Paul knew from first-hand experience Timothy's expertise - **in serving**.
  Can others work closely like that with you - when you are in second fiddle position?

In a word, Timothy had the mind of Christ (v 5). Self took second place to Christ, His gospel, His people - and even to fellow-workers. Sadly there weren't too many 'Timothys' around for Paul to choose from. It would be a mistake to reassure ourselves too quickly that we are one of these rare characters ...

Who better to send as an example of Christlike humility for the Philippian believers to model? Who better to find out for Paul what he longed to know about the Philippian believers? Timothy would be able to see how they received this letter, and whether they were a humble, united church, shining with the gospel into the darkness around them.

And Paul knew too that the Philippian believers were concerned about **him** - *Read v 23, 24.*

Soon Paul hoped to be released, or at least to know what the authorities would do to him - who better than Timothy to bear the news to the praying Philippians.

A brother   *Philippians 2 v 25 - 30*

Can you make it to the workgroup on Saturday?

Old Mrs Ellen could do with some help with her housework. Any vounteers?

Yes, of course we would have been glad to help out, but 'other commitments' tend to spring readily to mind to avoid such jobs. But Paul's final example of Christlike humility is someone who was willing to take on that kind of job. In particular a long, gruelling journey of around 800 miles to bring the gift to Paul from the church at Philippi (verse 30).

Read today's verses.

Now Epaphroditus was returning to his own church (bearing this letter). But Paul hadn't forgotten what Epaphroditus had been so willing to do for him. No complaints from Epaphroditus, even though the trip had almost cost him his life! In fact his only concern seems to have been the anxiety he was causing the believers back at home (verse 26!)

Paul is not slow to recognise this kind of practical self-giving. The warmth of his appreciation for Epaphroditus comes over in the words he chooses to describe him.

BROTHER
FELLOW-WORKER
FELLOW-SOLDIER

Think through what each of these words tell us about Epaphroditus.

Is there any reason why they could not be used of you, if only you take on board v 3 - 5?

Don't miss what Paul is saying. Epaphroditus may have had no teaching abilities, no particular 'gifts', but to Paul **he was his equal.** Why? Because in very practical ways his own life came second to the work of the gospel (v 30).

It is all too easy to undervalue people like Epaphroditus. It reads as though Paul needed to encourage the Philippian believers to appreciate him for his true worth - *read the verses again.*

Call to mind the Christians you know who are like Epaphroditus. How do you treat them or think of them? Compare with the two things Paul tells us in *verse 29.*

Now read Romans 16 v 1 - 13.

I often wonder what title Paul would have chosen to describe me ...

No additives! *Philippians 3 v 1 - 6*

There was one group whose unChristlike, self-centred attitudes were a particular threat to the Philippian church;

Read v 1 - 6.

Paul himself had been an extremely proud man - with good reason he thought! No doubt many a Jew had been jealous of his noble background and great success!

Look again at what he could say about himself, *verses 4 - 6.*

> Seven things which he had believed would recommend him to God. Surely with all those qualifications God would be pleased with him ...
>
> Yet now he could see that not one of them could win him any favour with God.

Why is Paul writing like this? Why does he list all these 'qualifications' if he has come to see how useless they were to please God?

Read v 1 - 3 again. Because false teachers at Philippi were teaching that circumcision was necessary to please God.

Paul could see very clearly how misleading that was. He could boast not only of circumcision but of six other qualifications too - but they had all been totally worthless in winning him salvation. He had given up relying on any of them, because he had found the only Person worth having confidence in! The Philippian believers must be sure to 'rejoice in the Lord' **alone**, not to put their confidence in anything else.

Notice how Paul describes these false teachers - *verse 2.*

> *(Wild) dogs ... Evil workers ... Mutilators of the flesh ('the concision' A.V)*

Strong language - but it needed to be. If we are tempted to feel that Paul is being too aggressive, perhaps we have not fully appreciated the treachery and evil of this kind of false teaching.

Why is it so serious?

Because only Jesus can save. Circumcision may have seemed a tiny thing to get upset about, but adding **anything** to His great work of dying to save sinners, will lead people finally to damnation and despair.

Circumcision may not be the issue today, but it has plenty of modern counterparts. Christ, it is held, is central to salvation - but you soon discover there are these experiences or those rituals or that giving which are necessary before you can be counted as a true Christian.

Pressure will be put on us to join with such people in 'united' worship or evangelism. Paul's answer would have been pretty clear; but are we prepared to take as firm a stand for the gospel?

Holding onto rubbish?　　　　　　　　　　　　　*Philippians 3 v 7 - 11*

RUBBISH! That is what Paul now thought of all those things he used to be so proud of (see yesterday's notes).

Many people today are proud of their lives. They might not put it like that, but they would be deeply offended if you suggested there was anything lacking;

regularly attending church ... kind and helpful whenever there is someone in need ... generous with their time and money ... careful to do all the right things and to avoid all the wrong ones ...

Good things, yes, but as far as winning any favour with God goes, they are **useless**, because even our best efforts are riddled with our own sinfulness. It is like offering God rubbish. None of these things will get people one step towards heaven.

See Isaiah 64 v 6.

It is important to examine yourself - to make sure you are not clutching hold of any 'rubbish sacks' which you think God will be pleased with. Have you, like Paul, thrown all your own achievements on the rubbish heap so that you can grasp the real treasure, 'Christ Jesus my Lord'?

Read v 7 - 11. (It is well worth investing a few minutes learning this section.)

Paul knew that his own 'righteous' behaviour was worth nothing. He knew that only **Christ's righteousness** could make him clean and pleasing to God. Only Christ's perfect life and His death on the cross were acceptable to God.

How could Paul obtain Christ's righteousness? *Verse 9* tells us - **through faith**, by resting in Jesus as his perfect Saviour.

But Paul, for one, was not satisfied that he was clinging closely enough to Christ.

Read v 10, 11 again. Do we too want to experience more of:

- ❑ CHRIST'S RESURRECTION? - His powerful life, **conquering** our sin. *Romans 6 v 4.*
- ❑ CHRIST'S SUFFERINGS? - Experiencing some of His **pain** over sin and **rejection** by sinners.
- ❑ CHRIST'S DEATH? - **dying** to self and sin. *2 Corinthians 5 v 14 - 15.*

What a rich privilege to daily experience Christ in our lives! But even that was not enough for Paul - he had his sights on **resurrection**; to be with Christ for ever, **entirely** saved from sin and death (v 11).

Pressing on ...   *Philippians 3 v 12 - 16*

It was as if he were running a race. It was a race he had started when he first met Jesus, and now he is nearing its end. Paul is old now, but that is not slowing him down because it is as if he can make out the finishing line ... What does he say?

Read v 12 - 14.   ('Apprehend' means 'grasp hold of'.)

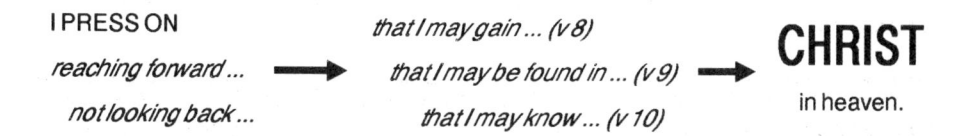

I PRESS ON	*that I may gain ... (v 8)*	
reaching forward ... →	*that I may be found in ... (v 9)*	→ **CHRIST**
not looking back ...	*that I may know ... (v 10)*	in heaven.

He had not got there yet, but he was reaching out to grasp the prize. Paul knew it was his - for Christ had grasped hold of him right at the beginning for that very purpose - that he might be able to 'take hold' of Christ, to know Him face to face.

But of course Paul was not describing his longing for Christ to show us what an outstanding Christian he was! No, this is to be the **norm**, for all believers to follow -

Read v 15, 16.

Maturity does not mean we have 'arrived'. Just the opposite! It is the mature believer who has the same mindset as Paul - who looks on life as a serious race, not a stroll in the country. Maturity means single-minded determination to press on to the arrival point - of perfection in heaven.

Yet Paul knows that most of us have not got so far as him in the race! We may still be fuzzy in our objectives, or cluttered by sins and hindrances that seem to cling to us. Don't be discouraged! Keep on the track that Paul has shown us, keep pressing on - and we will find God revealing to us more and more clearly the same goal.

Read Hebrews 12 v 1 - 15.

Enemies   *Philippians 3 v 17 - 21; 4 v 1*

Paul's letter to the Philippians is full of joy. Not even the threat of death itself can take away his joy. But in today's reading, Paul is actually **weeping!** Why?

Read all the verses to understand who are causing Paul such grief.

There are many people today like this. They call themselves Christian believers - but God calls them 'enemies of the cross of Christ'.

What are they like - so that we can be wary of them? Think carefully about the descriptions in *verse 19.*

These people do not have the mind that Paul has been describing. Their mind is fixed in the opposite direction; on 'earthly things'. And an earthly mind means an earthly lifestyle. They live not for the Lord Jesus Christ, but for their 'belly' - their own desires. They take delight ('glory') not in Christ but in conversation and company and entertainment they ought to be ashamed of. They will talk as if they are the most devoted of Christians, but Paul is clear; their destiny is in the same direction as their lives - 'destruction'. It is a horrifying thought, but does Paul's description here come uncomfortably close to home?

These are the kind of outgoing sociable types it is so easy to follow. Paul is **weeping** because he knows how potent a threat such people are to true believers. He means us to take him seriously and urges us to deliberately choose who we model our lives on (v 17). Paul says be sure to go along with those who are following his example.

Read Romans 16 v 17, 18.

How can Paul help these believers to stand firm? *Read v 20 - 21 again and chapter 4 v 1.*

By encouraging them to ...
-    **LOOK UPWARDS** (v 20). Also read *Colossians 3 v 1 - 3.*
  They have much greater, nobler aims in life because: 'our CITIZENSHIP is in HEAVEN' (i.e. that's where we belong).

-    **LOOK ONWARDS** (v 21). Also read *Colossians 3 v 4.*
  Jesus will come again - then they will be transformed, made holy like Him. All their struggles then will fade into insignificance.

Paul speaks with such certainty about these believers, his 'joy and crown'. Weak and vulnerable they may be, but he had no doubts about God's ability to bring them to glory (v 21).

So stand fast! (4 v 1) If 3 v 20, 21 is true for you, do not give an inch to the lures of the enemy!

Putting it into practice　　　　　　　　　　　　　　　　　　*Philippians 4 v 2 - 9*

'Standing fast' (v 1) sounds great in principle - but Paul needs to be more specific with us. What are the practical implications of much of what Paul has been saying?

RELATIONSHIPS *v 2 - 5*

Euodia and Syntyche could represent any two believers who are at odds with each other. Notice that whatever the rights and wrongs were, Paul's concern was to get the quarrel sorted out! If my nose has been put out of joint, so be it - it is far more important to get on with the work of the gospel together.

Once again, the key is **rejoicing in the Lord**. If He is 'always' the object of our attention and love, we will soon get on with one other. We will not be prickly and over-sensitive but 'gentle' (v 5); bighearted, meek, **Christlike** towards fellow-believers.

WORRIES *v 6, 7.*

'Don't worry!' Is Paul's advice just too unrealistic to take notice of? Everyone tells us not to worry, but it never helps a whole lot ... But Paul's is no throwaway 'there, there' - he speaks with the **authority of God Himself**. And, what is more, he has **God's answer to worry** to give us. We ought certainly to take notice - in fact we **must** take notice if we are Christians!

WORRY ⇨ PRAYER ⇨ PEACE

Peace is God's replacement for worry. Not an uneasy calm when all around us still rages, but the reality of knowing the God of peace is in command. And the route to this peace?
- Prayer! The kind of prayer that transfers the weight of worry to the One who has infinite ability to deal with it. *1 Peter 5 v 7.*
- 'Supplication', or 'petition'; specific request for God to do what is needed.
- 'Thanksgiving'; for God's faithfulness in the past - and for His goodness and willingness now ...

THINKING *v 8.*

We are responsible not only for what we do and say - but what we fill our minds with too. What are we feeding our thinking on (reading, T.V, conversations, music)? What does our mind drift onto when it gets 'free time'? Spend a while comparing your thought-habits with v 8. If you are to take this verse (and therefore the whole of Christian living) seriously ...
- What must go, because it is against / distracts / takes too much time from v 8?
- What will help you think more like v 8? (e. g. Bible study, time to meditate ...)

How true for you is *Psalm 119 v 97 - 104?*

DOING *v 9.*

They knew how to live - it was just a question of **doing it**. It is not enough to approve of what we are taught, or even to see it in action in others. The daily reality of knowing the God of peace is for **doers** of the Word.

Rejoicing in giving *Philippians 4 v 10 - 23*

The Philippians' gift had been a real encouragement to Paul. We can imagine his thrill at finding Epaphroditus knocking at his prison door with his love-gift. Yet it was not so much **that** joy which prompted Paul to 'rejoice in the Lord greatly'. What was it?

Read v 10 - 18.

❑   *'Not that I seek a gift'* (v 17a, 10 - 16)
Paul was certainly not ungrateful for their sacrificial giving, but he had learned the same attitude as Timothy - contrast ch 2 v 21. It was not his own comfort that was important to him, nor even the pleasure of knowing the love and care of the Philippian believers. No, Paul's joy was focussed on **the Lord**, not his own circumstances! That is why he could be content though shut away in prison. That is why the gift itself did not matter tremendously to him.

'The rare jewel of Christian contentment' is the accurate title of an old but excellent book. It is not every Christian who can honestly claim v 11 - 13 is their experience! We so easily pick up the attitudes of the world whose happiness goes up and down with the weather (and their bank-balance, popularity, T.V programme ...).

Just test yourself next time the washing machine breaks down and you have to do the week's washing by hand, or when the train is cancelled, or when it is raining on your holiday-in-the-sun.

Is your response just the same as unbelievers - COMPLAIN? Or are you CONTENT because Christ's grace strengthens you to 'rejoice in the Lord always'? (v 13)

❑   *'but I seek the gift that abounds to your account'* (v 17b, 18)
Paul was content for himself, but thrilled over what the gift would do **for the giver!** *Read 2 Corinthians 9 v 6 - 15.* And he was thrilled over what pleasure the gift had brought **the Lord** (v 18). Sacrifices are always well spent when they are offered up to God.
Yes, this was what had filled Paul up, and made him overflow with joy (v 18)!

We tend to get worried when people give us more than they can afford, but Paul had no such hang-ups. He knew for sure they could never be the worse off for it, for they had the God of *verse 19* caring for them.

What a promise! Giving is not risky! All of our needs put together can never begin to eat into the infinite resources of our God ...

Verse 20 is the right response - *read v 20 - 23.*

OUTLINE: Philippians - Christ-minded

'Let this mind be in you which was also in Christ Jesus.' (Philippians 2 v 5)

- Sum up each section in a short sentence or phrase (ideas below).
- Look for key words in each section (usually repeated).

SECTION	SUMMARY	KEYWORDS
1 v 1 - 2		
v 3 - 11		
v 12 - 18		
v 19 - 26		
v 27 - 30		
2 v 1 - 4		
v 5 - 11		
v 12 - 18		
v 19 - 24		
v 25 - 30		
3 v 1 - 11		
v 12 - 16		
v 17 - 21		
4 v 1 - 9		
v 10 - 20		
v 21 - 23		

Unity through humility ... greetings and grace ... pressing towards the goal ... striving together for the gospel ... Christ is preached ... working it out in the world ... no-one like Timothy ... enemies of the cross, citizens of heaven ... be united, rejoicing, praying, meditating ... opening greeting ... brother Epaphroditus ... rejoicing in giving ... everything but loss for Christ ... selfless choice ... Christ humbled Himself - God exalted Him ... thanksgiving and prayer

FACT - FILE : Colossians

> **COLOSSIANS**
>
> Fullness in Christ

THE CHURCH

- Colosse was an inland city in the Lycus valley in Asia minor (modern Turkey). See map on page 158.
- Colosse was a typically pagan city, with a large Jewish community; leading to a mixture of pagan and Jewish dangers for the new church.
- The church was not founded by Paul, but probably by some who visited Paul in nearby Ephesus around AD 55. (Acts 19 v 8 - 10)
- Epaphras was a key worker and minister.
- Colosse was where Philemon and (later) his slave Onesimus worshipped (See PHILEMON)

THE LETTER

- The author is the apostle Paul, writing from Rome from his house-prison.
- Written around AD 62, a few years after the founding of the church (at the same time as the letters to Philemon and Ephesus).
- Written to warn them against heresy brought in by false teachers, and to refocus them on Christ as their only source of life. (The heresy appears to offer them new, fuller experiences through a mixture of some or all of *false philosophy ... Judaistic ceremonialism ... angel-worship ... asceticism (mistreating the body to gain holiness)* - see especially Colossians 2 v 11 - 23.)
- The first two chapters display Christ, supreme, sufficient, against the background of false claims.

    The last two chapters show how to put a Christ-centred life into practice, in the church, home and world.
- See fuller outline at the end of the section.

If at all possible ...

Find time to read the letter through in one sitting, with this background in mind.

Be reassured!   *Colossians 1 v 1 - 8*

Perhaps you come out of doorstep encounters with Jehovah Witnesses or other such false teachers feeling that your faith has taken a bit of a battering. It's wise to go back to the solid truths of God's Word. What you have rested your salvation on is still there, unchanged - yet somehow it comes with fresh reassurance to calm your agitated mind.

Paul is very aware that the faith of the Colossian believers was being undermined by false teaching. Reassurance is called for.

1. Reassurance that the Colossians are true believers - *read v 1 - 5.*

- First there is a handful of separate words and phrases in v 1 - 3, all calculated to encourage. (Think about the **titles** Pauls uses for them, the **message** from God he brings them, the **actions** of Paul himself.)
- Then, Paul declares that three great proofs for assurance are firmly in place!

    FAITH centring in Christ.
    LOVE for fellow-believers.   Find the trio in *1 Thessalonians 1 v 1 - 5.*
    HOPE resting in heaven.   Is assurance the point here too?

It's worth using these three proofs to test the basis of our own assurance (or lack of it). Would Paul have been so confident about our FAITH if he noticed a careless unconcern for one another rather than LOVE, or an unhealthy focus on the here-and-now rather than on HOPE fixed on the glories to come?

---

2. Reassurance that the Colossians have received the true gospel - *read v 5 - 8.*

It is possible that the false teachers were sowing doubts about their minister, Epaphras. *Has he really preached the whole truth of the gospel?* No, the false teachers were claiming, there was a 'fullness' the Colossians had missed out on, which they were eager to supply ...

But Paul will have none of it. Think about these phrases:

- *'the truth of the gospel'* (v 5). Never separate 'truth' from 'gospel'. If our gospel messages are watered-down or disguised versions of the truth of God's Word, then we certainly open the door to those who claim to have more to offer.
- *'as it is in all the world'* (v 6). The same gospel everywhere! While sects and religions have minority or local appeal, the gospel of Jesus Christ is for everyone, everywhere!
- *'and brings forth fruit'* (v 6). It worked! The proof of the gospel's truth was seen in what it had done for them. And for us?

Others will be quick to entice you to new exciting experiences you have so far been deprived of. But, as we will see again in this epistle, such offers are false. Because they lead you away from the 'truth of the gospel' which cannot be added to.

Fully praying!   *Colossians 1 v 9 - 14*

We are rightly at home praying specifically for Mrs Jones' bad back, or for Brian to find a job. But how often do we pray urgently and specifically for our fellow believers like Paul does here? Paul's concern is such that nothing short of **unceasing** prayer will be frequent enough ...

Read v 9 - 11 in that light.

FULLY KNOWING GOD

We can be so negative and defensive about the supposed blessings we are missing out on. But Paul does not counter 'fullness' claims by saying 'we don't need that!' Instead he prays seriously that we might indeed be filled. Filled, not with something new, but with a fresh awareness of *what we already possess in Christ.*

- *Filled with the knowledge of His will (v 9).* For Paul that did not just mean guidance for the future! It meant knowing and doing God's will for us right now. We can be so concerned to know the way ahead that we forget that our greatest concern is to get on with what God has already made clear - living for Him in our current situation (v 10).
- *Increasing in the knowledge of God (v 10).* True believers won't be content to know God's **will**; nothing short of knowing God Himself will satisfy. And then they will want to know Him more ...

FULLY PLEASING GOD

It is one thing to know God's will, quite another to do it. That is why Paul prays for ...

- *all wisdom (v 9).* Wisdom converts knowing what we should do into putting it to practice in a hostile world. No wonder Paul needs to pray for **all** wisdom.
- *all might ... all patience (v 11).* Our concern is not only to fully please the Lord today - but to **keep on** pleasing Him, however hard the pressure is turned on. Defeated already? Yes, but for the infinite, inexhaustible supply that is ours - *'His glorious power'!*

Do you begin to see the need to make this kind of praying for each other a priority? After all, Mrs Jones back may never improve and Brian may remain unemployed for the rest of his life. But ultimately how much will that matter if they know instead the answer to the prayers of v 9 - 11?

Instead of an extra reading, look - or should I say pray - closely through those verses once again.

But Paul is far from finished. He knows how to thank God, as well as what to ask Him for.

Read v 12 - 14, taking each phrase slowly, and turning it, if you can, into your own praise to God, for His glorious blessings in Jesus.

Supreme over all   *Colossians 1 v 15 - 20*

*'Consider the **supremacy** of Christ and you'll not need to be convinced of His **sufficiency** for you.'*

Paul's purpose in these breath-taking verses is practical. It is not simply to exalt Christ in our thinking - but in our living too! But if we are to even begin to take in the wonder of the verses we must do a little work ...

> ❑ **READ** through *v 15 - 20* a few times.
> ❑ **NOTICE** 'all things' is repeated 6 times. What points are being made?
> ❑ **COMPARE** *v 15 - 17* with *v 18 - 20*. Spot the similar phrases as Paul parallels *Christ's supremacy over creation* (v 15 - 17) *with Christ's supremacy in redemption* (v 18 - 20).
> ❑ **STUDY** some difficult phrases:
> - 'image of the invisible God' (v 15). Jesus is not less than God; He is God **revealed** to us.
> - 'firstborn of every creature' (v 15). Not that Christ was the first created being. John tells us He existed *'in the beginning'*. No, Paul means that Jesus is the heir; He has authority over every created thing. *Read John 1 v 1 - 3; Psalm 89 v 26 - 29.*
> - 'firstborn from the dead' (v 18). Heir not only of creation but of salvation too; risen to be the source of all resurrection power.

SUPREME OVER CREATION - *read v 15 - 17*. Christ...

IS BEFORE all things (v 17)
CREATED all things (v 16)
IS OVER all things (v 15)
SUSTAINS all things (v 17)
IS THE PURPOSE for all things (v 16)

Nothing exists without Christ! Not only did He make all things, but the universe would collapse instantaneously without His power holding it all together.

Isn't the Christ who holds the universe in His hands sufficient to meet every single need of our own?

SUPREME IN REDEMPTION - *read v 18 - 20*. Christ...

HEAD over all His people (v 18)

SOURCE of all God's fullness (v 19)

RECONCILER of all things (v 20)

Nothing exists in Christ's Church without Christ! There is no other authority - Christ alone is the HEAD, ruling His people. There is no other SOURCE of blessing - God has nothing for us outside of Christ. There is no other way of salvation - all who will be RECONCILED will find their peace only in the 'blood of the cross'.

Jesus Christ is Lord. God's determined purpose is that 'in all things (among all His creatures) **He** might have the pre-eminence'. Own Him then as supreme Lord of your life!

YOU He has reconciled! *Colossians 1 v 21 - 23*

The last section should have left us open-mouthed; humbled and amazed by the glory and supremacy of Christ. Yet Paul is coming to something designed to leave us even more astonished and full of praise ...

It was YOU that He reconciled! Read v 21 - 23.

ENEMIES - *v21*

Many would resent this description. They would say they had nothing against Jesus - and might even claim to be His friends. Yet it is not so much our **words** that give the true picture, but our ...

- **mind.** Do we have the mind of Christ - or of the world? Do our attitudes, our values, our chosen thoughts conflict with popular opinion - or with Christ, as found in the Bible?
- **works.** Actions also speak louder than words. Unless all we do has been brought under Christ's rule, His blunt view of our lives is 'wicked' - however decent we may think them to be.
  Matthew 25 v 41 - 46 makes searching reading.

Besides, it is not only a question of our attitude to God - but of His to us. We are 'alienated', because His anger with our sins can never go away until we are ...

RECONCILED - *v21.*

If I wrong you then it's my job to do the reconciling. But praise God that **Christ** is the one who reconciles, when it is we who have caused the alienation! We have spent our lives in determined opposition to Him - and His response? To lay down His life in determined love, to make peace with His enemies!

BLAMELESS - *v22.*

Isn't that even more amazing? That we, habitual, obstinate sinners, should be presented blameless before the holy Judge! Yet no charges can be brought. Christ has already paid all the penalties for His people's sin. And not only blameless, but holy too! How can we ever thank Him enough for such indescribable love!

CONTINUE - *v23.*

Paul leaves no room for any who think reconciliation means relaxation. Far from having a careless approach to sin, reconciled people are to **continue** ...

- 'grounded and settled.' Shift ground from the foundation of Christ and we are sure to sink.
- 'not moved'. Many will try to lure us away from our 'hope'. Many will persuade us that we can have all the blessings **now.** But reconciled people know that their hope is of glory **to come.** That is worth holding on for in faith!

Authentic minister   *Colossians 1 v 24 - 29*

Paul hated drawing attention to himself, but he also knew that you can't separate the message from the messenger. Was his message authentic? Was it from God? Paul gives some thought-provoking marks of a genuine minister of God. Let the Colossians, and let us, use them to distinguish the true teachers from the false -

Read v 24 - 29.

THE SUFFERING
v 24

Paul does not celebrate his wonderful successes, his heavenly experiences or his prodigious gifts. No, it is **suffering** that he will rejoice in, because suffering brings him closest to his suffering Saviour. Of course Christ's atoning sufferings are fully complete, but His sufferings **in His church** on earth have yet to be filled to the brim. Do you, like Paul, count it the deepest joy to share like this in Christ's sufferings? *Philippians 3 v 10.*

THE COMMISSION
v 25 - 27

Paul had no problem defining his commission ('dispensation'). It was purely and simply to *'fulfil the word of God'*: God had chosen to unveil the 'mystery' of salvation - and God had chosen Paul to do the same! Paul's task was to make all of God's truth fully clear, to broadcast the whole message of the gospel. And yet, however clear the message, it is only God who can 'make known' the 'riches of the glory' to people blinded by their sin (v 27).

THE PREACHING
v 28

We have already noticed briefly **what** Paul was to do - but how was he to do it?
- Warning. Positive messages are not sufficient!
- Teaching. Emotional appeals are not sufficient!
- Wisdom. That disqualifies all who do not seek all wisdom from God.

And his aim? Simply more converts? No, Paul had not finished with his converts until they were perfect, **every one** of them. Are we too preoccupied with **conversion** to take care over **completion**?

THE LABOUR
v 29

The first three marks make the fourth inevitable. If a minister is not agonising in hard labour, then he is not being faithful to his commission. Yes, it is **God's** power that must be at work, yet it is by the sweat and toil of God's servants at work that His 'working' or energy is powerfully seen. If we want God to work with energy, then we too must be prepared to work with energy.

Authentic? By these tests Paul stood out a mile as God's own minister. But we must apply them to our own day, and our own churches ...
Read 2 Corinthians 4.

Burden for souls?   *Colossians 2 v 1-5*

Do you have a 'burden for souls'? A question that rightly bothers believers - but how often do we feel convicted over a lack of real care over **saved** souls as well as lost ones?

Read about Paul's burden - *v 1 - 5.*

It is no cosy interest Paul describes - but a battle. He is in bitter conflict, struggling against the enemy of souls for the survival and growth of these believers. And when we consider that he had never met most of them, doesn't it show up how feeble our 'burdens' are even for the closest of churches?

Read about Paul's burden for another church - *1 Thessalonians 3.*

So what was Paul's burden for these believers?

- **Encouraged hearts.** This is vital; heavy, discouraged hearts are easy meat for the enemy. Without encouragement the Colossians would soon be listening to the tempting offers of false teachers.
- **Loving unity.** Not merely a friendly peacefulness; they needed to be 'knitted' or 'welded' together in the kind of love that **committed** themselves to one another.
- **Assured understanding.** A firm grasp of spiritual truths was high on Paul's list of priorities for these believers. Have we lost sight of how crucial this is if we are to stand firm?

We can all see that these would be nice, even important, to have - both for ourselves and our fellow-believers. But aren't they ideals which, realistically, we can scarcely hope to know much of?

Categorically not! Believers already have in their possession the Source of everything they need ...

'CHRIST, in whom are hidden all the treasures of wisdom and knowledge'

Hidden, not from us, but **for** us! God has stored priceless treasures up for us in Christ, yet they mostly lie untouched, unwanted, unasked for - while we struggle manfully on with our own resources ...

Read v 4, 5 again. Are you in danger of being enticed - because you are dissatisfied with your Christianity? It seems dull, insipid, lacking direction and unfruitful? You long for a breath of fresh air?

Then, says Paul, go back to Christ for all the treasures you need! Like the Colossian believers so far had done, stand firm in Him against all tempting offers.

Fullness in Him　　　　　　　　　　　　　　　　　　　*Colossians 2 v 6 - 10*

Is it enough to counter attractive new offers of spiritual fulfilment by gritting our teeth and clinging on to the status quo? 'We must stick to the Word of God' we tell ourselves (and so we must), so we resign ourselves to the struggle and routine of our admittedly humdrum Christian lives ...?

Paul would have groaned at that approach! Yes, hold on to the roots, *because you need them for GROWTH not just existence!* Counter the false claims with vibrant, growing experience of Christ.

Read v 6 - 10, then focus on v 6, 7 using the comparison below.

THE PAST	THE PRESENT
Received Christ ...	So walk in Him!
Rooted in Him ...	So be built up on Him!
Taught the faith ...	So be established in the faith!

For true believers, **THE PAST** is not in question (whatever doubts and fears they sometimes have). That has indeed happened, praise God! But are we still living in the past? Are we standing still rather than walking on with Christ? Are we stuck on the foundations rather than growing into a useful building? Do we still need to be taught the basics, or are we becoming firm and established in God's truth?

And there is one more key to spiritual fullness - *'abounding in thanksgiving.'* If we are truly filled with the Spirit we will be full to bursting with gratitude to God. Our attention will be turned away from ourselves and our experiences, to praise the Christ to whom we owe all.

And **Christ** is where Paul focuses us yet again - *v 9, 10.*

IN HIM the infinity of God meets sinful mankind. If we want spiritual fullness, there it is - all the vastness of God Himself. Concentrated, as it were, in Jesus - for us.

IN HIM you are already full! We who have Christ possess fullness! We need no special teaching to learn the 'secret'. We simply need to go to Christ to enjoy it. It would be well worth taking time to turn Paul's prayer into your own - *Ephesians 3 v 14 - 21.*

Centred firmly on Christ we are in a position to combat error, however enticing - *v 8.*

Their higher knowledge or philosophy is in reality hollow deceit compared with Christ. Their human traditions, their principles based on this world's thinking, are never to be bartered for the fullness of Christ's presence that He alone can give us.

Fellowship with Him *Colossians 2 v 11 - 15*

'In Him' was the little phrase that kept cropping up in the last section - FULLNESS **IN** CHRIST.

'With Him' is the key phrase in *v 11 - 15* (see v 12 (twice) & v 13), shifting the emphasis to FELLOWSHIP **WITH** CHRIST.

YOU WERE CIRCUMCISED! *v 11*

They did not need the physical circumcision the false teachers were requiring - they were already circumcised with the only circumcision that counts! Their physical bodies had no need to be cut about - Christ had already severed the 'flesh' of their old sinful nature!
Fellowship with Christ means separation from sin

YOU WERE BURIED! *v 12*

Think back to your baptism - what did it symbolise? That when Christ died, you died, so far as the reign of your old sinful nature is concerned; that when He was buried your sins were buried with Him, to be held against you no more.
Fellowship with Christ is sharing in His death.

YOU WERE RAISED! *v 12*

It was as if your old self had died - but you were not left in the grave. Just as Christ was raised to life, so you were given a new life to live for Him. Through faith in God's power to raise the dead you are united to the risen Saviour.
Fellowship with Christ is sharing in His resurrection power.

YOU WERE MADE ALIVE! *v 13 - 15*

Paul expands on that last point. What was tied up with raising sinners to new life?
- **Forgiveness from sin.** Notice 'all' trespasses'. Not one will be held against us.
- **Freedom from charges.** Only the blood of Christ could blot out the condemnation of God's Law on us. But not only have our charges been cancelled, we have been freed from its demands!
- **Freedom from evil powers.** Satan can still plague us, but he can no longer enslave us.

Fellowship with Christ is sharing in the freedom of His life.

Our fellowship with Christ is all based on what He has already done! Never undervalue it! Never forget what He has made you! Never stop praising Him for it!

Read Ephesians 2 v 1 - 15.

Let no-one defraud you!   *Colossians 2 v 16 - 23*

Self-discipline is one of the notable absences in Christian living today; yet without it we can expect to make little progress in godly living.

But if anyone suggests that full spiritual experience can only be gained by keeping to their particular rules or 'guidelines', we are to resist it tooth and nail! What is sold as moving out into new and exciting reality is in fact moving backwards not forwards.

That gives us a framework for understanding this section. *Read the section through* a couple of times.

Now we will take a closer look at Paul's evaluation of this new teaching;

- **It takes you back into the shadows (v 17).** Certainly the old Jewish ceremonies had a value - they were like shadows that prove there is something real to look for! But that 'something real' had come! Whoever will want to substitute his glorious Saviour with legalistic regulations?

- **It disqualifies non-takers (v 18).** They were running well, but now these people would disqualify them from the prize - on the basis of not knowing the secrets of self-humiliation and angel worship.
  Always beware of a superior super-spiritual attitude that puts others down.

- **It disconnects you from the Head (v 19).** That's the fatal flaw! Without a living growing connection to Jesus we can achieve nothing - and we can't even survive ourselves.
  Read Jesus' teaching on that - *John 15 v 1 - 8.*
  Don't be tempted by exciting church-growth figures. Verse 19 makes it clear there is only one kind of growth that is worth having - the increase God gives us through living on the Vine.

- **It subjects you to men's commands (v 20 - 22).** Men start to take over the headship that belongs to Christ. Severed from Him we become slaves again to man-made regulations. The 'prophecies' or 'words' of mere men take over from the loving commands of the Saviour.

- **It fails to achieve its own goals (v 23).** The wisdom and effectiveness of the methods may appeal at first glance - *but you can't kill off sinful desires by a system of self-discipline.* Outwardly it might be impressive, but so far as God is concerned it is of no value. Just as many monasteries turned into dens of iniquity, merely restraining our **outward** indulgence will turn our hearts into cans of worms.

'Let no-one defraud you', says Paul. Hold fast to your glorious Head, following Him in voluntary, loving, self-disciplined obedience. That is the way to grow!

A matter of life and death *Colossians 3 v 1 - 7*

So what is the way forward? We have learnt in chapters 1 and 2 that it can only be found **in Christ**, and to resist the offers of short-cut merchants who can offer us spiritual fullness by other means.

Now, in chapters 3 and 4, Paul brings it home in practical application. If you want to know how to grow up into Christ, then here it is ...

Read v 1 - 7.

A matter of life ... *(v 1 - 4)*

- ❑ *Remember the life you have!* We seem so quickly to forget that Christians live now in heaven's kingdom, not earth's. Paul tells us ...
  ... we have been raised to a new, **heavenly** life (v 1) ...
  ... our life is bound up with Christ who is reigning **above** (v 3) ...
  ... that our destiny is life in **glory** (v 4).

  We are not talking about life in the future, but here and now. Therefore ...

- ❑ *Nurture the life you have!* It is no use thanking God for giving us new life and then getting on with living our old earth-centered lives. We are actively, seriously to ...
  ... seek the things that are above (v 1) ...
  ... set our minds on things above (v 2)

  Why can we be so concerned about the world's business (which we have died to - v 3), and so little interested in heaven's affairs (where we belong for ever)?!
  When we are free to think our own thoughts, our aims and minds are to be heaven-bent not earth-bound. Jesus' own life flatly contradicts the idea that we can be so heavenly-minded as to be no earthly good ...

... and death *(v 5 - 7)*

- ❑ *A command! (v 5).* Since our sin threatens to kill our spiritual life, we must kill sin. Not merely keep it under, but do away with it. We need ruthlessly and systematically to do battle with all remaining 'members' that belong to our earth-bound nature.
- ❑ *A warning! (v 6)* If your sin never knows your wrath against it, then you must face God's wrath turned against you.
- ❑ *A reminder! (v 7)* That is how it used to be before. But there has been a radical change - you have already died to sin (v 3), so how can you let it live in you?

So it is hard. Yes, and life-long. There are no short-cuts to enjoying the full blessings of life with Christ. But there is no other way to holiness - or to heaven. In a real sense it is a matter of life and death ...

Read Romans 6.

Put off ... put on   *Colossians 3 v 8 - 13*

In the unlikely event of my becoming royalty overnight, one thing would certainly have to change. My wardrobe. All the cheapie half-worn-out clothes would have to go, and be replaced by high quality brand-new outfits that would live up to my new status.

That is the kind of reasoning behind this section; but with one difference. It is because we **already have** changed our wardrobe that we are urged to **carry on** throwing out the old and choosing the new;

> *Put off - because you already have put off!*
> *Put on - because you already have put on!*

Follow that argument through as you *read v 8 - 13*.

Notice that Paul's topic is our **public** wardrobe; it is all to do with how we treat each other as Christians ('blasphemy' v 8 AV, NKJV probably means insulting **each other** rather than God, to fit with the context.)

> Contrast the behaviour of the 'old man' in v 8, 9 with that of the 'new man' in v 12, 13. The temptation is to skim through lists like these, but we need to chew over each item in turn, examining ourselves as to how we can in practice 'put off' or 'put on'.
>
> Which of the new are in particularly short supply?

A few points from the centre section help us in our application:

- **The standard to follow is Christ, not others!** Don't take a look around and conclude you are doing quite nicely compared with the shoddy dress of other Christians. It is **Christ's image** that believers are being turned into - *v 10. See 1 Corinthians 15 v 49.*

- **We are not to be choosy over who we are Christ-like towards!** Our unity is to **bridge all barriers**, whether racial, religious background, cultural, or social - *see v 11.*
Christ is all that matters - if we have Christ then nothing must divide.
1 Corinthians 12 v 12, 13, 25 - 27.

- **It is not optional!** Notice how v 12 puts it; God's people are His elect; **chosen** to be holy, **chosen** in His love, **chosen** to put on the Christ-like characteristics of v 12, 13. If God has specially selected us to be like this, how can we resist Him ...?
Read Deuteronomy 7 v 6 - 8.

Five pillars of unity   *Colossians 3 v 14 - 17*

Unity is not the same as lack of disunity. This section does not show us how to avoid falling out with each other, but how to be **bonded together in a working partnership for God**.

Paul gives us five massive pillars on which unity will stand or fall. And be sure to notice that he doesn't present them as nice suggestions, but as binding commands from God ...

Read v 14 - 17.

LOVE v 14

In a sense you can forget the detailed lists Paul has just given - so long as you take on board this one word, **love**. Everything else will follow if you *'love one another as I have loved you'.* But then again you need the lists, because love must saturate every area of our lives together; then it becomes that unbreakable bond knitting us to each other.

Read 1 Corinthians 13 v 1 - 8.

PEACE v 15

God's peace must rule **in our hearts** before it can rule **in our church** (the 'body'). If we are at odds with the Lord we can expect to be at odds with each other. Think of the ways peace is threatened in your own heart, and in the life of the church. How are we to obey God's command to see to it that His peace is ruling?

GRATITUDE v 16, 17

Why does Paul need to repeat this two or three times? (See end of v 17) Is it because we are so forgetful to be thankful, so inclined to take everything for granted? (The psalms are an antidote; e.g *Psalm 107 v 1, 2, 8, 15, 21, 31*)
And is it because thanking and praising God for His marvellous grace towards us is **so uniting**? We forget our petty gripes once we join in thanksgiving to our glorious God!

WORD OF CHRIST v 16

Never think you can create unity by undermining the pillar of Christ's word! Yet it is not enough for the Word to rule over us - it must **dwell in us**. Is Christ's Word always 'at home' in your life, there in all that you say and do? And is it there in an ever-increasing **richness**?
Once Christ's Word has enriched us, its richness can infect our church. What unity that brings!

NAME OF CHRIST v 17

With the first four pillars in place, we are ready for united **action**. But how? Only in 'the name of the Lord'. With His authority, for His glory, through His **power**. And not only the major events, but simply everything we do, or even say. If we want unity, we would be wise to apply these tests...

At home, at work *Colossians 3 v 18 - 4 v 1*

Paul does not mean us to leave behind v 8 - 17 as we move into the specific instructions of today's section. Rather, he is making sure that we don't forget to apply them to individual people! Read those verses again so they are fresh in your mind, before tackling *3 v 18 - 4 v 1*.

WIVES - HUSBANDS - v 18, 19.

Before wives begin to feel their shackles rise at the unwelcome instruction to submit, we should **all** pause a moment to submit. For our attitude towards today's verses is a litmus test of our attitude towards Christ. Do we willingly bow to Him as our Master, receiving His teaching as His messages of love for our best interests? Are we glad to reject the unbelieving world's values and wear the badge of 'Christian, servant of Christ'?
That badge isn't a lot easier to wear for the husband. For love means not merely treating your wife as equal, but honouring her **above** yourself! And just as the wife is to submit to the husband when he is demanding and even unreasonable, so the husband is to love her in her most difficult and stubborn moments.

CHILDREN - PARENTS - v 20, 21

The world's harsh values have moulded us here too. Lest we should imagine that our responsibilities to our parents do indeed end at 18, *read 1 Timothy 5 v 4, 8, 16*. Notice how the phrase 'good and acceptable before God' (v 4) mirrors Colossians 3 v 20.

But again Christ's standards are no easier for fathers (and mothers). Yes, children can be cowed into submission by sheer force. But the Christian method is the force of love and patience; discipline must always be to build up, not destroy. And any Christian parent will tell you how taxing that proves to be.

SERVANTS - MASTERS - 3 v 22 to 4 v 1

On the surface this is more relevant for some cultures than others. Yet the principles can easily be transferred to any work situation - and should certainly be applied to all who count themselves as followers of the Servant - King. Whatever the area of application, the key point to remember is this; *Christians have been set free to serve Christ!* It may well be hard to put your heart into that pointless, wearisome task for an ungrateful boss, it may well be difficult to resist the temptation to slacken off when he is not around - **but will you do it willingly for Christ?** That gives it a point and a joy; for He is always watching, to reward you with that smile of approval ...
Once again it's all too easy to slip by the testing requirements for 'Masters'. Not just fair pay, but all the respect and appreciation and warmth that is due too. In a word, to do to others as your loving heavenly Master does to you.

> Compare with Paul's expanded teaching in *Ephesians 5 v 21 - 6 v 9;* many new points come out.

Five points of evangelism!   *Colossians 4 v 2 - 6*

How can we best evangelise? A question that will keep cropping up so long as we care about lost souls and the kingdom of Christ. Paul gives us a basic outline for spreading the gospel (though of course these principles can be applied to other areas too);

Read v 2 - 6 and work through the five key pairs.

- *prayer and thanksgiving (v 2).*
  Paul urges us to *continue*... but do you know how hard that can be? You pray on and on without results, your faith gradually evaporating until you are ready to give up. Paul has an antidote;
  - *thanksgiving.* For Jesus, for the gospel, for His promises, for your own salvation, for opportunities - and for answers. Thanksgiving fuels faith.
  - *watching.* Watch out for the devil's tricks to discourage you. And watch, expectantly, for answers to prayer. It's sure not to be long before you have still more to thank God for.

- *open doors and closed prisons (v 3).*
  Pray for opportunites! The doors may be locked as tight as prisons, but Paul knows God can open locked doors - and He can provide other open doors, even while we are still banging against the old locked ones ...

- *I ought to speak ... you ought to answer. (v 4, 6).*
  Notice the distinction. Preachers who God has appointed ought to be **preaching the gospel** - that's God's main method of evangelism. The gospel that is a mystery to so many 'ought' to be made clear - pray for that!
  But most of us are called to be 'responders' - not preachers. We are called to be ready, keen to respond to remarks and questions, thankful that they have noticed the difference between our life and theirs.

- *wisdom and urgency (v 5)*
  Wisdom is not a kind of cold-water treatment for zeal, to tone it down and give it balance. True wisdom towards unbelievers is to be burning with true zeal, 'buying up every opportunity' to turn them from their hell-bent career. Foolishness and cowardice are words for the kind of 'wisdom' that always waits for a more convenient season to tell them the gospel.

- *grace and salt (v 6).*
  A salty grace is needed! Not weak and timid, insipid as an egg white - but with a flavour that makes people sit up and take notice. Grace that has **salt** will not only be sensitive to the needs of your friend, but **probe** those needs. Not only respect them as people, but **search** them as sinners. It will not only faithfully present the gospel, but bring it relevantly **home** to them.
  See it in Jesus Himself - *John 4 v 6 - 26.*

How can we best evangelise? Remember Paul's principles and you won't go far wrong.

Family bonds   *Colossians 4 v 7 - 18*

'Give our love to everyone.' You may sometimes end your letters like that, but Paul does not do that here. Greetings are not tagged on the end as a throwaway gesture of friendliness; they are an important part of what he has to say.

Why? Because Paul has grasped what it means to belong to the **family of God**. Notice the family, sharing kinds of word (brother, fellow-) as you *read v 7 - 18*.

Three factors seem to be especially important in the bond between Paul and his brothers in Christ;

COMMUNICATION v 7 - 9.

Paul often went to great lengths to pass accurate information between him and the churches - usually by means of a trusted friend. It wasn't just so that they could pray meaningfully for the 'great apostle' ; no, he was intimately concerned with their needs too. Paul was never too busy to be interested; it was a genuine two-way relationship.

> Is our problem the opposite of Paul's? Drowned in communication, as the pile of prayer-letters stacks up along with the phone-bill? The danger is that we spread our concern too thinly, so that communication is too superficial and too rushed to build up our bonds in the gospel.

LOVE

'Beloved brother' (v 7, v 9), 'beloved physician' (v 14) are descriptions showing just one way Paul shares his feelings. But see how the whole section breathes genuine warmth and concern throughout. He didn't have to struggle to find the energy to think about these fellow-believers; it was spontaneous love that made him care.

> Love is God's gift - but it is one we are to cultivate to enjoy close family relationships. In what ways are we to do this? (e.g. commending others rather than criticising (v 12, 13), thinking of others' needs (v 10)).

LABOUR v 7, 9, 11 - 13

Notice how Paul keeps repeating the themes of faithfulness, serving, labour and zeal. There is nothing that bonds Paul closer to his brothers and sisters than to know they are 'fellow-workers' in the gospel he so loves. To think of the few who he can rely on to be rock solid in their prayers for him and their labours for Christ, gives him the deepest joy.

> When Paul talks of fellowship, he is not thinking of sharing food and fun - but sharing in labour and giving. Do we need to revise our ideas of what will truly unite us? *Read Philippians 1 v 3 - 8* as an example.

OUTLINE: Colossians - fullness in Christ

> 'As you have therefore received CHRIST JESUS the Lord, so walk IN HIM, rooted and built up IN HIM and established in the faith, as you have been taught, abounding in it with thanksgiving.' (Colossians 2 v 6, 7)

☞ Sum up each section in a short sentence or phrase (ideas below).
☞ Look for key words in each section (usually repeated).

SECTION	SUMMARY	KEYWORDS
1 v 1 - 8		
v 9 - 14		
v 15 - 20		
v 21 - 23		
v 24 - 29		
2 v 1 - 5		
v 6 - 10		
v 11 - 15		
v 16 - 23		
3 v 1 - 7		
v 8 - 17		
v 18-4v1		
4 v 2 - 6		
v 7 - 18		

Burden for steadfastness ... Giving thanks for their faith ... Preaching, towards perfection ... You He has reconciled ... Praying for fullness ... Living evangelistically ... Christ supreme in Creation, redemption ... Complete in Christ ... Let no-one lead you into the shadowland! ... Life hidden with Christ ... Put off, Put on ... Living it out at home and work ... Family greetings ... Alive with Christ

FACT - FILE : 1 Thessalonians

> 1 THESS
>
> Encourage!

THE CHURCH

- Thessalonica is still a city in Greece. At this time the population was mainly Greek, but with other nationalities including Jews, who had a synagogue there. See map on page 158.
- The city was located in a key position on the 'main road' to Philippi, and also a major port. Therefore it was a busy trading centre.
- The church at Thessalonica was founded by Paul on his second missionary journey. Many Greeks were remarkably converted, and some Jews too, before intense persecution from jealous, unbelieving Jews forced him to leave (Acts 17 v 1 - 9).
- Paul moved on to Berea, then to Athens, but was very anxious about the new believers in Thessalonica. Hindered from visiting them himself, he sends Timothy to encourage them. Upon Timothy's return to Paul now in Corinth, bearing good news, Paul wrote this first letter to the Thessalonians.

THE LETTER

- Written by Paul from Corinth, on his second missionary journey, around AD 52.
- Written to
  - encourage the persecuted believers to press on with the remarkable faith, love and courageous witness they were showing.
  - counter rumours and misrepresentations about his own ministry
  - correct mistaken views concerning the second coming,
  - exhort the believers to holy, moral living and caring fellowship.
- See fuller outline at the end of the section.

If at all possible ...

Find time to read the letter through in one sitting, with this background in mind.

Transforming power | *1 Thessalonians 1 v 1 - 5*

Humanly speaking a Christian church in the middle of heathen Thessalonica was distinctly vulnerable. And when you add to that the kind of vicious persecution from the Jews that Paul had experienced, you can begin to grasp the pressure they were under. *Read Acts 17 v 1 - 9.*

Right from the first sentence Paul is out to reassure them! *Read v 1 - 5.*

- ❏ *You are the church in God and in Christ* (v 1). That was how they should see themselves. Not the church in antagonistic Thessalonica, but the church in the perfect security of God Himself!

- ❏ *We are always giving thanks for you and praying for you* (v2). Not only was God looking after His own church, but Paul was caring for them too - and Silas and Timothy. Who can tell the power of continual, joyful prayer for believers who we know are under pressure?

- ❏ *It's real* (v 3). They hadn't been conned. It wasn't a mere change of religion in a moment of pressure. The reality of their transformation proved that they could not just give up their new-found faith:
  - *a faith that is proved by works.* It wasn't a new set of beliefs alone - it was a new life.
  - *a love that is proved by labour.* It is one thing to say that you love, another to love.
  - *a hope that is proved by perseverance.* They had not given up! Why? Because their confidence was based on a risen and reigning Saviour. Whatever the persecution they couldn't give up the certainty of salvation!

- ❏ *God has chosen you* (v 4). It wasn't their choice of God that counted, but His choice of them! And He would not change His mind when the going got tough; His love was determined to see them through. Not that Paul had a special revelation about the Thessalonians. It was simply that there was no other explanation of v 3 - their lives proved God had chosen them ('your election'). And there was no other explanation of v 5 either - the gospel had come to them with God's transforming, choosing power.

- ❏ *The gospel came in power* (v 5). They knew it had not been an emotional 'trip'. Plain, ordinary words, without any hype, had become dynamite to them. God had spoken and they knew it. It was nonsense to suppose they had been drawn by the magnetism of a man - they knew full well how genuine and straightforward Paul had been.

Work through the points to apply them personally. Do you have grounds to be reassured and encouraged to press on?

And, having been encouraged ourselves, let us plead with fresh energy and faith for God to come like this again and again. That He will indisputably transform lives by His power alone, through plain preaching of truth.

The gospel does not stop here!   *1 Thessalonians 1 v 6 - 10*

It is not surprising Paul was overjoyed when he thought of the Thessalonian believers. *Read v 6 - 10* and you will quickly see why ...

Receivers

become

Transmitters

Not only had the gospel come to them with God's power - they had received it with God's joy! (v 5, 6). And while today there seems so much 'joy' that is 'worked up' and superficial, there is no question about the source of the joy that springs up out of severe persecution - 'joy of the Holy Spirit'.

The gospel message didn't terminate at Thessalonica! They sent it beaming out not only in their own region (the whole of Modern-day Greece), but far beyond too (v 8). We can imagine they made full use of the strategic position of Thessalonica (located on main trading routes for both sea and road), exploiting every opportunity to spread the word far and wide.

There is surely a challenge here. If the Thessalonians, despite cruel opposition, despite a complete lack of our modern resources, could find ways to achieve v 8, is it really beyond us? If we have received, let us ask God for courage and wisdom to use all available opportunities and resources to transmit the message that has changed us. But, of course, it is not only a matter of spreading the **word** ...

Followers

become

Examples

What does greater harm to the cause of Christ than 'Christians' who are all mouth? 'Christian' means follower of Christ; and that is precisely what the Thessalonians were (v 6). And they had translated that 'ideal' into practical, everyday Christ-like living - by copying the example of a real live Christian.

Verses 7 - 10 are impressive indeed. Their success in spreading the message was startling enough, but their **changed lives** had become even more notorious! What were the features of their faith that made such an impact on other believers?

- **New purpose (v 9).** Perhaps we are used to thinking of this verse as a summary of true conversion, but think through why it carried such a punch. Is your life so radically different from others, not only in actions but **purpose,** that it challenges the meaninglessness of their existence?
- **New prospect (v 10).** Would others guess this is what we are waiting for? Does our message fall on deaf ears because we are obviously more concerned about the here-and-now than the hereafter...?

We can imagine how encouraged the Thessalonian believers would have been by this first chapter. Paul was right; their faith **was** real, and it was working! Read Jesus' own encouraging message to witnessing Philadelphia - and His warning to lax Laodicea - *Revelation 3 v 7 - 22.*

God-pleaser *1 Thessalonians 2 v 1 - 6*

Most of us are only too quick to jump to our own defence, but for Paul something infinitely greater was at stake than his own reputation. If the messenger was discredited then the message would be too. To defend the gospel, to defend the faith of the Thessalonians, Paul must defend **himself** from the slander of the enemy.

Read v 1 - 6.

The key is in v 4. Why had Paul's visit not been 'in vain' (v 1), but produced the lasting effects of chapter 1? Why hadn't he given up after being knocked around at Philippi, but had the courage to face the antagonism of Thessalonica? (v 2)

Because he was a God-pleaser, not a people-pleaser.

It was **God** who had commissioned him, **God** who had trusted him with the gospel, **God** who was testing his heart to see if he would remain faithful (v 4). So what men (or even Paul himself) thought of him was pretty irrelevant ...

In theory we would obviously agree with Paul. No, it really does not matter what people think, so long as we are pleasing God. But sadly, in practice pleasing men often wins the day. To help turn theory into practice ...

Think: What truths should we keep reminding ourselves of?

e.g. God is watching - v 4

Notice the principle of *Matthew 6 v 2;* read *10 v 24 - 39.*

'The fear of man brings a snare, but whoever trusts in the Lord shall be safe'. (Proverbs 29 v 25)

That key affected everything. With it Paul could defend himself against a whole string of accusations ...

- **No deceit** (or error) v 3. Paul had honestly declared nothing but the truth.
- **No impurity** v 3. Motives were pure; the apostles were after neither money nor following.
- **No guile** v 3. No methods designed to 'catch' the audience.
- **No flattery** v 5. Paul was always positive and encouraging, but cared enough for their souls to tell them home truths.
- **No greed** v 5. There was no pious facade covering up a heart that was out to get what it could.
- **No position-seeking** v 6. Yes the apostles certainly should be honoured - but they didn't seek that for themselves.
- **No self-assertiveness** v 6. They had no desire to put the Thessalonians under the 'burden' of the apostolic authority, exerting their power over them.

Paul could say all that with a clear conscience - confident that the Thessalonians, as well as God, knew it to be true.
Use the list to test your own sincerity in being a God-pleaser.

All-round ministry — *1 Thessalonians 2 v 7 - 12*

So Paul was not the self-seeking imposter his opponents made him out to be. But what **was** he like? Paul gives five areas in which to assess his ministry. *Read v 7 - 12.*

How he CARED v 7

I wonder if we would be surprised if we could meet the apostle Paul. His letters come over so powerfully that he cuts a rather awe-inspiring figure. But those who knew him didn't find him threatening. Like a mother tenderly caring for a baby, he lovingly watched over the Thessalonian believers, guarding them from danger, providing for all their needs.

Those of us who share Paul's forceful character should take note - and pray much for the 'meekness and gentleness of Christ'.

How he GAVE v 8

True care for others results in two gifts not one. We may be willing to share the gospel of God, because that's free - but giving our lives costs. Think that through in your own situation. How far are you prepared to go in giving not just your time or money, but your energy and commitment?

How he LABOURED v 9

Paul would far rather **bear** a burden than **be** a burden. And if that meant hard manual labour over tents then Paul was ready for it - so long as he could preach the gospel at no charge to the hearers.

Overloaded? Working all hours of night and day? It's worth it - so long as it is for the gospel ... Let's not think of easing our own burdens when it means becoming a burden to others.

How he BEHAVED v 10

They were watching and God was watching. Both how 'devoutly' he worshipped God and how 'justly' he treated people. Paul certainly did not claim to be perfect, but his conscience knew there was no reason to point a finger at him.

Both sets of eyes are upon us too. What is their verdict?

How he TAUGHT v 11, 12

Paul didn't only care for them as defenceless babies (v 7), but as maturing children too. And that meant teaching them with all the variety of encouragement, instruction and motivation of a good father. Paul knew that just as natural children need training, so spiritual children do not automatically 'walk worthy of God'...

Is v 12 your goal - both for your own life and that of others? What consequences should that have?

Read Paul's testimony to the church leaders at Ephesus - *Acts 20 v 17 - 38.*

Faith that survives 1 Thessalonians 2 v 13 - 20

A few years ago there was a series of science programmes called 'Take Nobody's Word For It'. Although it had been necessary for Paul to defend his own ministry amongst the Thessalonians, he could afford to breathe a huge sigh of relief. They had not taken **his** word for it - it was **God's** message they had received!

Read v 13.

Why should people believe your words or mine? Why should they be persuaded that our views of life and salvation are right while thousands of other views are wrong? Why should they ditch their own beliefs, change their whole way of life and trust their eternity to the scheme they have been told by a person as fallible as themselves?

Don't let them take your word for it. Otherwise next week they'll be taken in by someone else more convincing but wrong. We can only afford to rejoice like Paul when we are sure they are not trusting in our beliefs but God's truth.
How might that affect your approach in sharing the gospel?

Faith in God's Word works. Just how robust such faith is can be seen in how it fares under persecution -

Read v 14 - 16.

Let's not underestimate the strength of the opposition. The same Satan that inspired the Jews to kill the Lord Jesus, the same Satan that hired Gentile Thessalonians to wipe out this young church, is just as keen to neutralise us. Sometimes the means he employs are more subtle - but only so that we will remain blissfully unaware of his purpose. Be sure of this; he is still out to win us back to himself. And not only that, he is still out to prevent us spreading the gospel further (v 15, 16).

Yet the focus of these verses is not so much on Satan, but the people he uses. God's awesome wrath is **already resting** on all who oppose the gospel (v 16). (Just as it was hanging over the Jews, ready to be unleashed in a few years time - in A.D. 70 when Jerusalem would be destroyed.) The Thessalonian believers needed to remember that when they wondered how they could go through with it; God was on their side, and He was against their enemies. Contrast *Revelation 12 v 12, 17 with Revelation 11 v 16 - 18; 16 v 1 - 7.*

It is easy to see why Paul was anxious to visit these believers. In fact he was almost bursting with longing to encourage them! Notice the intense, emotional words he uses in *v 17 - 20.*

Of course he would have been accused of ditching these Christians. But there was a very different reason why Paul had not visited them. The same Satan that was at work in Thessalonica was desperate to stop Paul from counter-attack! (v 18)

Satan does hinder. But it's worth reflecting on the poor success he had at Thessalonica. Chapter 1 shows how good God is at spreading His gospel, despite Satan's worst efforts...

Mission Timothy   *1 Thessalonians 3 v 1 - 5*

Another glance at the end of chapter 2 will give us a measure of Paul's commitment to these believers - *read v 19, 20 again.*

If you are a Christian, what crown of joy are you looking forward to? Surely to see your Lord face to face! *But even that wasn't all Paul had his sights on.* The prospect of seeing his hopes fulfilled for these Thessalonians, that he might fully give glory to God for them - that was the joy he had in mind here! That was how much they mattered to him.

Paul had not given up hope of seeing these Christians before then (as we will see in 3 v 10, 11), but for the time being he had to send Timothy in his place;

Read 3 v 1 - 5.

What was Timothy's brief?

1. TO STRENGTHEN THEIR FAITH v 2.

Paul did not argue that because they had started well they could carry on pretty much on their own.

Young believers need nurturing if they are to become firmly established in God's truth.

2. TO ENCOURAGE THEIR FAITH v 2 - 4.

'Encourage' or 'comfort' is a key theme in this letter. Yes, Paul had warned them it was going to be tough, but warning on its own is not enough to see them through! Timothy would be able to reassure them that nothing had gone wrong - rather it was just as expected!

Our duty is not done when we warn seekers or new believers about the cross they must bear. We must get alongside them and see them through the hard patches (and not only young believers either).

Jesus warned of trial - but He also promised the great Encourager; *John 16 v 1, 4; 14 v 16 - 18.*

3. TO KNOW THEIR FAITH v 5.

It is not clear how much Paul had heard about the Thessalonians before Timothy reported back. Certainly he had seen God powerfully at work at the beginning - but he also knew how effective Satan's temptations can be. He wasn't simply going to assume that all was well! He was determined to do all he could to prevent that initial faith and zeal giving way under pressure.

It is no good simply hoping for the best, or leaving it to God to look after new Christians. If we care like Paul, we will not be able to rest until we are sure all is

Thrilled by their faith   *1 Thessalonians 3 v 6 - 13*

We might have thought Paul would have been so preoccupied with the difficulties and demands of Corinth (v 7, *Acts 18 v 1 - 6*) that he would have little time and energy to spare for the Thessalonians - especially as he knew that Timothy was with them.

Far from it! Paul's intense concern over these believers gives us some useful tests of our own care for others -

Read v 6 - 10.

- distress over the danger they were in (v 7 probably includes both Corinth and Thessalonica)
- longing to see them and encourage them (v 6, 10)
- his own spiritual life affected by their condition (v 8)
- overjoyed at the news of their love and faith (v 9)

What a boost the Lord gave His faithful servant by this news! (Compare with a later concern for the Corinthians themselves - *2 Corinthians 7 v 5 - 7, 13.*) The Lord does indeed know how to encourage His people.

Notice though that Paul's relief and joy only served to fuel his longings for the Thessalonians! *Read v 10 - 13.*

- **prayer that he might see them** (v 10, 11). The news of their faith had been very good - but Paul would not rest till it was fully mature! Not that this was the only reason for his prayer. Besides the fact they needed teaching, Paul **loved** them and longed to have time with them again. How we need to watch against an attitude that sees people as 'cases' needing our help, rather than individuals who we love.
- **prayer for their growth** (v 12, 13). In his absence, what was Paul's great desire for them? What will keep them most securely? What will do them most good?
  LOVE. This was already a strong point (4 v 9, 10), but you can't 'increase and abound' too much in love!
  What would love do for them? Notice the sequence:

         LOVE ⇨ STRENGTHENED HEARTS ⇨ HOLY LIVES

Think through the ways in which love for one another achieves this.

So Paul might never be able to visit the Thessalonians, but Jesus was certainly coming! When He comes for us, will He find our lives established in holiness? (v 13)

Come clean!   *1 Thessalonians 4 v 1 - 8*

Paul changes tack, but not subject. In the first three chapters he has skilfully demonstrated his genuine joy over their faith, and deep concern for their growth. Now, in chapters 4 and 5, he builds on that platform. He **exhorts** them to 'abound more and more', and **teaches** them in some areas of deficiency. *Read v 1 - 8.*

Sadly we can begin to understand the immoral air these believers breathed in heathen Thessalonica. It was not surprising there were problems in the area of sexual purity - yet neither was it excusable.

- *they had received this teaching* (v 1) Paul had been perfectly clear about it in his brief time at Thessalonica.
- *they ought to live to please God* (v 1) Screamingly obvious, yet even Christians can forget how impossible it is to please God in **anything** while indulging **one** sin. Do you covet Enoch's testimony? *(Hebrews 11 v 5).*
- *they knew God's commands* (v 2) To argue that God's clear moral commands in the Bible do not apply to us today is as dishonest as it is treacherous. Paul certainly did not adapt God's commands to the permissive society of Thessalonica ...
- *they knew sanctification was God's will* (v 3). Praise God that He accepts sinners in all their filth. But that in no way means it is acceptable to go on living in filth.

No excuse, but that does not mean it is easy. To combat sin we need to see it in its true light - and that is how Paul helps us here:

- *it is a question of honour* (v 4). The original word is 'vessel' ('wife' NIV) and seems to mean in the Bible one's sexual drive. This, Paul says, is to be controlled. We are to treat it as God's gift, with 'honour', with care and dignity.
- *we are no longer ungodly* (v 5). Those who do not know God are controlled by their lusts. But God's children are not to follow them. We are no longer slaves to sinful passion!
- *we are cheating a brother* (v 6). Not only God but a fellow-believer was being wronged (by illicit relations with his wife or daughter). And remember, God is on his side, jealously angry for him...
- *we are denying our calling* (v 7). God called us to holiness at the same time as He called us to salvation! Have you forgotten that you can't have one without the other?
- *reject this and you reject God* (v 8). We are not free to have our own view on this. It is not man's opinions but God's command. And to reject God's command is to reject God Himself.

Paul does not baldly state the facts. He lovingly urges them and exhorts them - and as he does so he knows he has the Lord Jesus with him (v 1). Will you listen, brother or sister?

Read 1 Corinthians 6 v 9 - 20.

Increase in love!   *1 Thessalonians 4 v 9 - 12*

There is one sure way of avoiding the problems of v 1 - 8. **Brotherly love!**

Read v 9, 10.

If Paul has no need to talk to them about brotherly love, then why does he?!

1. In **general** their love was impressive, and widespread, so Paul has no need to say much about it. But there were some specific areas it had not yet filtered through to (e.g. v 1 - 8 and possibly other situations Paul knew of but does not refer to). Let their love so abound as to affect **everything.**

Will you respond to Paul's tactful exhortation? How he encourages us, instead of justifying our current level of love, to examine every nook and cranny of our lives to see if love is abounding as much as it could ...

2. There is always room to **increase** in love. And it is not only those who are lacking who need to listen, but those whose love is already a talking point.

Those who love most are those who already see how valuable love is. Growing in love is already a priority for them ... And for you?

3. The greatest love still needs keeping alive. They would soon grow complacent about it unless they were urged to keep looking for more!

If we are not increasing in love it is likely that we are decreasing. And we are not to leave the exhorting to the minister!
Consider Hebrews 10 v 24, 25.

Brotherly love is relevant to the next topic too - *read v 11, 12.*

It's easy to gather that it was their keen interest in the Lord's return that caused a distinct lack of concern about earning an honest wage. But a moment's thought would have shown them how selfish that was. Brotherly love does not lead to ...

- **fanaticism.** Zeal stirs others to godliness. Fanaticism agitates others to restlessness. Be zealous - but 'calm'.
- **interfering.** As the saying goes, Satan soon finds work for idle hands to do.
- **laziness.** It is not spiritual to be occupied with spiritual thoughts or spiritual talk, when we should be earning a wage.
- **sponging.** That seems to be the thought of the end of v 12. We should not need to depend on others.

Not only does this kind of attitude damage fellow-believers; it brings the gospel into disrepute too (v 12).

I often hear of unbelievers put off by the lives of Christians; but is it you and I who are doing the putting off ...?

If we see the seeds of those sins in our lives, let us respond straight away. Not all the Thessalonian believers did, and the issue became more serious -
Read 2 Thessalonians 3 v 6 - 15.

Encourage with the truth!   *1 Thessalonians 4 v 13 - 18*

The Thessalonian believers had really got hold of the truth that their Lord was coming back for them. They lived watching and waiting, in a way that many of us neglect. But their expectancy was tinged with sorrow and confusion; what would happen to believers who had already died? Would they somehow miss out on the glorious resurrection?

Read v 13.

Ignorance always does damage. Some people think that it is not so important what precise truths the Bible teaches; the great thing is to live as a Christian. But just as a hazy understanding about Jesus' return caused the Thessalonians unnecessary grief, so will any area of ignorance damage our Christian living. Poor teaching means poor living.

So what are the facts about our Lord's return that would encourage these believers - and us? *Read v 13 - 18.*

1. *When Jesus comes, He will bring the deceased believers with Him (v 14).* Notice the lovely way he describes them - they are **asleep in Jesus.** There is no need to grieve over them as you would unbelievers, for they are perfectly safe resting in their Saviour. And their resurrection is just as sure as Jesus' own, because they are inseparably united to Him.

2. *The 'dead in Christ' would in no way be disadvantaged (v 15 - 17).* (The word 'prevent' or 'precede' in v 15 probably refers to order of advantage rather than time.) Rather than being forgotten, their bodies would rise first to join Christ in returning for those still alive.

3. *All believers 'asleep' or alive will share in the glory of that Resurrection Day (v 16, 17).* We can be so side-tracked by the details of the precise order of what will happen, that we miss its glory. The shout, the archangel, the trumpet, the clouds - all pointing to the majesty and finality of our Saviour's return. No believer will miss its glory then; all without exception will be safely gathered by Christ to be with Him for a glorious eternity.

Read Matthew 24 v 26 - 31; 2 Thessalonians 1 v 7 - 10.

Paul's teaching would surely be a great relief to those who were mourning over their loved ones. **But the teaching must be kept alive - v 18.** God's truth is not to be put on a shelf as soon as we have grasped it, but continually applied to our lives. And that means comforting and encouraging **one another.**

What will we do when we see Christians whose lives do not square up to God's Word? Leave them to their ignorance, and let them and others suffer the damage? Or gently get alongside them and encourage them with the truths in the Bible?

The Day of the Lord   *1 Thessalonians 5 v 1 - 5*

When would Jesus come again? Such was their interest in the subject that it is possible they had asked Paul to throw some light on the question. But Paul had none to throw; they knew all there was to know about the time of Jesus' coming.

Yet they still had lessons to learn about **how to live** in the light of the Lord's return -

Read v 1 - 11, focussing especially on v 1 - 5.

It is worth thinking about the way Paul describes Jesus' coming;

- *'as a thief in the night'* No warning, sudden, unexpected - and unwelcome for those who are not prepared. What are the lessons? - *Matthew 24 v 42 - 44.*
- *'sudden destruction'* That is what is least expected. Never have people been so concerned about security for this life and so indifferent over security for eternity. They are as oblivious of their danger as those in Noah's time; *Matthew 24 v 37 - 39.*
- *'as labour pains'* When they come they come! However inconvenient, the pains of birth cannot be put off. People may put off thinking about it, but they cannot put off the Day God has appointed. And they will be as helpless to escape its anguish as a woman in the throes of labour.

Then there will be no possible escape. How we need to keep the awesome realilty of this coming event at the front of our minds. It will be too late then to warn our friends and neighbours to be prepared for eternity.

But for ourslves, if we are believers, the picture is in complete contrast. The brightness and glory of His coming holds no threats for those who are eagerly waiting to be transformed into His likeness. Does Paul's description hold for you?

- *'not in darkness'* Translated into the kingdom of light! No longer living in the realm of the darkness of sin and unbelief, but governed by new principles.
- *'sons of light'* Belonging to the same family as **the** Light of the world. Lives marked by purity, openness and beauty, having nothing to hide under the cover of darkness.
- *'sons of the day'* Notice the play on words. The Day ushers sons of the day into an eternity of daytime.

The application is obvious - and Paul develops it in the following verses (see next section);

If this is true of you, then live like it!

Be ready! 1 Thessalonians 5 v 6 - 11

Jesus is coming! But will we be ready? More to the point, are you ready today?

Paul spells out for us what that means. *Read v 5 - 11*, then compare with the table to see the contrasts:

CHARACTER (v 5, 8)

CHARACTERISTICS (v 6 - 8)

CONSEQUENCES (v 9)

of the night	*of the day*
sleep	*watch*
be drunk	*be sober*
wrath	*salvation*

To be ready means ...
- **WATCHING not SLEEPING.** Like those waiting eagerly for the Bridegroom, not those who really could not care less. How sleepy and indifferent we can grow, as He seems so long coming - but you want to be ready, don't you? ...
- **SOBER not DRUNK.** It is as though unbelievers are in a drunken stupour. Living for the now ... careless about the 'morning after' ... oblivious to danger ... laughing at the warnings. That is what it is like to belong to the 'night'; but we are no longer like that, are we? (v 5). Instead we are to be alert, thoughtful, serious, ready at any time.

Rather like a sentry on guard. And ready not only in the sense of watching, but **prepared for attack.**

What is the armour we need to defend ourselves against Satan's arrows? *v 8.*
- **FAITH.** Our strength is in Christ. We can resist the devil only because He did. But we will only be ready if we are still depending on Him.
- **LOVE.** Satan is expert at prising open a chink of resentment to stir up a world of bitterness. And then we will not be ready ...
- **HOPE.** Do not be distracted by enticements around. The way to be ready is to keep looking forward to Him coming!

Looking to CHRIST, to OTHERS, to HEAVEN is the surest defence against the enticements of SIN, SATAN and the WORLD.

Again, how we need to encourage one another to remember that Jesus is coming again (v 11)! But praise God that **He** has not grown careless, or forgotten His purpose for His people! As certainly as He has died for their sins, and obtained their salvation, so certainly will He come again to have every one of them live with Him for ever!

Read v 9, 10 again.

Jesus' teaching is just the same - but in parables; *Luke 12 v 35 - 48.*

Internal affairs *1 Thessalonians 5 v 12 - 15*

The headings in some Bibles of 'various exhortations' or 'final instructions' are not terribly helpful here. Paul is not shooting off random exhortations, but giving us careful guidelines first for our relationships within the church (v 12 - 15), then concerning our walk with God (v 16 - 22).

HONOUR YOUR LEADERS! (v 12, 13)

It is easy to pick holes, to find fault with their weak points and gripe over what they fail to do or will not allow you to do. But how often do we stop to **appreciate** what they actually do (v 12), and to **highly value** them because they are engaged in the greatest work in the world (v 13)? Love them for it, says Paul!

To help us, he describes them as ...
- **labourers.** Do you thank God for those who toil over your soul night and day?
- **overseers.** They are over us in authority, so respect them. And over us in care, so love them. But either way they are only 'over' to watch and guard, not to 'lord it over' us.
- **admonishers.** Literally they 'put us in mind' to obey God's ways. Remember how difficult that can be and be ready to respond to reproof rather than defend yourself.

And one last point (v 13). One of the best ways of showing that you care about your leaders is to care about one another! Nothing is so draining for a pastor than bickering and tension among the believers. Nothing more encouraging than to see them growing together in peace and purpose. Which links to the following verses ...

CARE FOR ONE ANOTHER! (v 14, 15)

In a sense all believers are to be 'overseers'. Don't leave it to the pastor to lovingly watch over one another! Especially we have responsibility for the ...
- **unruly.** Surprising, perhaps. We tend to steer a wide berth and leave it to the leadership! But a careful word from 'within the ranks' can be far better than the elders exerting their authority.
- **fainthearted.** Literally 'little souls'. Do not leave them to drop out of the race; encourage such to take heart and press on.
- **weak.** They need help, not criticism! Get alongside and steer them away from temptation and sin. *Read Romans 15 v 1 - 7.*

So we are to watch thoughtfully and prayerfully for special needs. But there is something everyone requires from us. Patience! We all **cause** pain to other, so let us **take** it patiently too. The world hits back when mistreated, or ignored, or taken for granted, but God's people have a far more effective method *(v 15)*. In other words ...

'Overcome evil with good.'

Read Romans 12 v 16 - 21.

All, always and in everything!   *1 Thessalonians 5 v 16 - 22*

There is no problem in **understanding** v 16 - 18; they are as clear as the sun. The problem comes in taking them seriously; surely they cannot mean what they say ...?

But, lest we should conclude he is exaggerating, Paul backs up these startling messages by assuring us that they are **God's will for us all**, not just some pie-in-the-sky ideal.

Since God means us to take Him seriously, spend a while reflecting on the impact they should make on your life:

1. Rejoice always.
There would be no point in saying it at all if he did not mean **always**. Nobody needs telling to rejoice when they feel like it! It is those times when we are at rock bottom that we most need the reminder. We must take our eyes off our misery, stop focussing on all the reasons we have to be sad, and look upwards. Then we will see that there is plenty still to rejoice about!

    Rejoice always because there is always reason to rejoice!

Think through what some of those reasons are.

2. Pray without ceasing.
As soon as we stop looking to the Lord in anything we do, prayerfully depending on Him, then we start to lose the battle. (Remember Moses' battle with Amalek? *Exodus 17 v 8 - 13.*)

Apply it more specifically too; never **give up** praying about a particular thing, never **despair** of an answer, never **stop committing it all** to the Lord. If He says do not stop, it is because He means to answer!

3. In everything give thanks.
Whatever trial you are 'in', do not forget to thank God that you have such a loving, faithful, powerful God to be in it with you. Think what it would be like with no God, and surely you will want to give thanks?

Still on the theme of our relationship with God, Paul continues - *read v 19 - 22.*

The whole section seems to be about our attitude to **God's words**. Instead of **despising prophetic utterances** because of so many false prophesies, thus **quenching God's Spirit**, they were to **test the prophecies, holding fast** to what was good and **holding off** ('Abstain', 'Avoid') what was false.

[While that seems to be Paul's thrust, he puts it in very general terms. Why? So we can apply the principles to many areas of our lives! How do they speak particularly to your own situation?]

God's revelation is now complete. We have no need of further prophesies or words from God. But we may still extinguish the Spirit by failing to take on board His Word as it is preached to us - or by eagerly accepting all teaching without holding it up to the test of the Bible.

Find the marks of true teaching in *1 John 4 v 1 - 6.*

Turning to God *1 Thessalonians 5 v 23 - 28*

Paul has finished exhorting the Thessalonians, but he has not finished. He knows he is powerless to make them respond!

So he turns to God. *Read v 23, 24.*

- **The God of peace.** The God who **loves** peace and who **gives** peace. The God who is grieved when we are agitated or unsettled like some of the Thessalonians, and the God who makes us calm and stable, resting in Him. *Read 2 Thessalonians 3 v 16.*
- **The God who sanctifies.** Be holy! That has been Paul's message to the Thessalonians, and God's to us. And yet, because Paul knows how powerless we are to make ourselves holy, he urgently calls on God to do this work in us - to perfection. And He will! *Philippians 1 v 6, Leviticus 20 v 7, 8.*
- **The God who is faithful.** What a tremendous relief to be able to commit these dear believers to a supremely faithful God! Paul has done what he can, but now he can rest them all on the God who cares far more than he does. He will preserve every one of them for the day when Jesus returns to bring them home.

If you care about your brothers and sisters in Christ will you exhort them? (v 11, 14) And if you care enough to exhort them will you not pray for them, trusting God to do what only He can?

And remember, we are to exhort one another as brethren, not inferiors! The church is to be a partnership not a hierarchy. Paul, despite his apostolic authority, is anxious to underline this;

read v 25 - 28.

- **Brethren pray for us.** We have no need to be afraid of asking our **brethren** (and sisters of course) to pray for us! It shows that we need them and value them.
- **Greet all the brethren.** Paul is sending his greetings - not to some, but every one of the believers. And, whatever the 'holy kiss' means for us today, our greetings must be **warm** and **holy**. They are to carry a special message that we belong to one another as brothers and sisters in Christ.
- **Read it to all the brethren.** Paul solemnly adjures them to do this - because the very ones who most need it might be less than keen to listen! But even these are brethren - and 'holy' ones at that.

What is it that unites us? Grace! We are all nothing in ourselves. Everything we possess and have become is through sheer grace. Think for a moment about the last verse.

OUTLINE: 1 Thessalonians - encourage!

'But we urge you, brethren, that you increase more and more ...'
(4 v 10)

- Sum up each section in a short sentence or phrase (ideas below).
- Look for key words in each section (usually repeated).

SECTION	SUMMARY	KEYWORDS
1 v 1-4 v 5-10		
2 v 1-12 v 13-16 v 17-20		
3 v 1-5 v 6-10 v 11-13		
4 v 1-8 v 9, 10 v 11, 12 v 13-18		
5 v 1-11 v 12-15 v 16-22 v 23-28		

Jesus coming to gather dead and alive ... increase in love ... children of day ... evident salvation ... prayer for the church ... overjoyed at Timothy's news ... called to holiness, not uncleanness ... committing each other to the Lord ... Rejoice! Be sensitive to the Word! ... sent Timothy instead ... honour leaders, encourage one another ... power that transformed ... giving the gospel, giving himself ... good witnesses by good work ... persecuted for the Word of God ... Paul's longing to see them

FACT - FILE : 2 Thessalonians

> **2 THESS**
>
> Stand fast!

THE CHURCH

- Thessalonica is still a city in Greece. At this time the population was mainly Greek, but with other nationalities including Jews, who had a synagogue there. See map on page 158.
- The city was located in a key position on the 'main road' to Philippi, and also a major port. Therefore it was a busy trading centre.
- The church at Thessalonica was founded by Paul on his second missionary journey. Many Greeks were remarkably converted, and some Jews too, before intense persecution from jealous, unbelieving Jews forced him to leave (Acts 17 v 1 - 9).
- The growing faith, love and evangelistic zeal of the Thessalonians, despite ongoing persecution, was a cause of special joy to Paul. But, in spite of Paul's first letter there were still some problems, largely springing from wrong ideas about Jesus' second coming.

THE LETTER

- Written by Paul from Corinth, on his second missionary journey, around AD 52/53 - fairly soon after his first letter.
- Written to encourage them to stand firm in the faith despite persecution, looking for Jesus to come with justice. However they must remember that Jesus will not come till after the 'man of sin' has been revealed. So they are to hold fast to the truth, continuing to work calmly and admonishing any who refuse to.
- The theme throughout revolves around the Second Coming. Thanksgiving, encouragement, teaching, exhortation and prayer are interspersed.
- See fuller outline at the end of the section.

If at all possible ...

Find time to read the letter through in one sitting, with this background in mind.

Painful progress   *2 Thessalonians 1 v 1 - 5*

Perhaps you have reached a bit of a plateau in your Christian life. You might not have identified it as a plateau; certainly you are not too concerned, as things seem to be ticking along nicely ...

The example of the Thessalonian believers is designed to jolt us out of any complacency -

Read v 1 - 3.

Their great faith was growing exceedingly! Their great love was abounding!

> Paul's first letter shows their love and faith already to be impressive (1 v 8; 4 v 9, 10)

Paul had not been complacent - and now his prayers were answered! (1 Thess. 3 v 12)

They had not been complacent - they had responded to exhortation! (1 Thess. 4 v 9, 10)

And what made their growth even more startling was all the disadvantages they were up against. Little teaching ... no-one to nurture them ... heathen culture ... fierce persecution; and yet progress was in leaps and bounds!

> I think of a believer admitting that the world gets the better of him, and that his faith splutters along unhealthily. And yet, when challenged, he rather shrugged his shoulders, pointing out the pressures and loneliness he faced. *How can I be expected to grow in this environment?*

No wonder Paul is **compelled** to give thanks! He cannot contain his joy over these choice believers. So much so that it seems he can hardly keep quiet about it ... *read v 4, 5.*

Remember the Thessalonians, Paul might say, *the pressures they face are enormous, but their faith is standing firm.*

> We might ask whether our example would be an encouragement to others - or best not mentioned ...

Paul might be overjoyed over their faith, but it is doubtful if **they** were! Would they last out against the onslaught? Would their faith survive? Paul helps them see things from a different viewpoint in v 5;

The way God is helping you endure is a clear sign of His judgement on those who are persecuting you.

God never ignores the way unbelievers attack His people. Never think they are getting away with it, at your cost.

And that means not only righteous anger for those who oppose Him, but also righteous reward for those who suffer for Him.

Those who suffer for the kingdom of God are those who are counted worthy of it.

Read Matthew 5 v 10 - 12. Contrast with *Matthew 10 v 37, 38.*

Coming in glory   *2 Thessalonians 1 v 6 - 12*

How certain is it that God will see his people through persecution?

> As certain as He is righteous! v 6
> As certain as Jesus is coming again! v 7

It is not that God is doing His people a favour in rescuing them from attack - His own justice is at stake! His justice demands trouble for those who trouble His people - and rest for those who are troubled. That justice is hidden for the moment, but it will be dazzlingly revealed upon Jesus' return ...

Read v 4 - 10.

Awesome division. It is hard to imagine how two views so radically opposite will exist together. One man will be ecstatic with joy and wonder while his neighbour will be calling for rocks to fall on him to cover him from the wrath of Jesus Christ. But the two reactions can only exist together for a moment. The same glory that captivates the adoring eyes of the believer will banish the unbeliever to everlasting destruction.

The pressing question is what **our** response will be. Many make the hopeful assumption that all will be well, many foolishly maintain that it is impossible to tell what the future holds for them. But the verses are very clear ...

-    **'who do not know God ... who do not obey the gospel'** *v 8, 9.*
  It is no neutral issue as to whether we know God, by responding to Jesus' command to repent and submit to His lordship. If we will not yield to His message of love and forgiveness we will not be fit to enter God's presence. We will be shut outside to face His everlasting righteous anger. Never imagine that God is indifferent to our response; for Jesus' coming will make it awesomely clear how much He cares.

-    **'His saints ... those who believe.'** *v 10.*
  Do both descriptions fit you? Many **claim** to believe, but only the changed life of a 'saint' (= 'set apart person') shows genuine faith. Jesus will receive no admiring gazes from those who have indulged in sinful living; His holiness will not delight them but consume them. But notice that 'believing saints' will not only see His glory; His glory will be **seen in them!** God's glory will be seen above all else in the millions of lives redeemed through the Lord Jesus.

Is it any wonder then that Paul turns to prayer? How he longs for this prospect of glory for the Thessalonian believers. So he prays that **now**, in their lifetime, God might be glorified through holy, devoted living. For only if he is glorified in us now, will He be when Jesus comes again ... *read v 10 - 12.*

Read 2 Peter 3 v 8 - 14.

Man of sin   *2 Thessalonians 2 v 1 - 5*

Dr Martyn Lloyd-Jones said he could always guarantee an increased turn-out by announcing that his subject would be 'the last things'. We need to watch that our fascination for the unknown does not lead to unhealthy speculation or lopsided preoccupation ...

Apparently the church at Thessalonica was buzzing with excited rumour. Paul was not sure of the source, whether it was by 'spirit' (prophecy?) or some supposed message or letter from himself, but it was a rumour that he needed to firmly quash -

Read v 1 - 5.

Don't get agitated so quickly! A moment's quiet reflection would have stopped them jumping on the latest second-coming bandwaggon. They would have remembered Paul's clear teaching (v 5) that categorically ruled out the possibility that Jesus had already returned.

We are always to stop, remember and pray before jumping. Whatever the teaching, or scheme, or event, see how it squares up to what you know God's Word teaches.

Paul mentions two things in particular which they knew must happen before Jesus comes;

1. Falling away v 3.

The best comment is *Matthew 24 v 10 - 13.* There will be widespread desertion of the faith by professing Christians. True believers will endure to the end and be saved, but the visible church will by and large abandon the faith.

And this movement of apostasy will have a leader ...

2. The Man of sin will be revealed v 3, 4.

Though there are many who have the spirit of antichrist, the language here points to a specific person, the Antichrist, who will be clearly seen just before Jesus' second coming. Notice his chrracteristics:

- He delights in **sin**.
- He **opposes** God.
- He **exalts** himself above God.
- He **proclaims** himself as God.

Many have been dubbed as the Antichrist, but we are told he will be 'revealed'. Surely when he comes it will be painfully obvious to true believers,

The language in these verses seems to be borrowed from some difficult verses in Daniel. *Read Daniel 7 v 25; 8 v 9 - 12; 11 v 36, 37.*

The primary meaning of these prophesies has been fulfilled - in a notorious forerunner of Antichrist, Antiochus Epiphanes. Shortly before Jesus' **first** coming this evil man caused havoc amongst God's people, desecrating Jerusalem's temple by sacrificing on a pagan altar which he erected over the altar of burnt-offering.

Jesus insists repeatedly that we are to watch, to be ready for His sudden return. But He also promises us clear signs preparing us to look up and see our redemption drawing near. Only if we are ready for Christ will we be ready for the fierce onslaught that will precede His return.

Satan's masterpiece? *2 Thessalonians 2 v 6 - 12*

As Paul continues his description of the 'man of sin' or the 'lawless one' ('wicked' A.V), we begin to realise that the Thessalonians had an advantage over us! They knew just what Paul was meaning, but we have to struggle a bit.

Read v 6 - 12.

Q. *What is the mystery of lawlessness?* (v 7)

A. We can easily see that there is a spirit of lawlessness at work around us. But the 'mystery' hidden from us is the power that brings about that lawlessness. This mystery will be unveiled in the revealing of the 'lawless one', who is lawlessness personified.

Q. *What is restraining this lawlessness from being revealed in the 'lawless one'?* (v 6, 7) ('let' A.V means restrain)

A. The Thessalonians knew, but we do not! Whether it is a person or an influence the original does not make clear. Ultimately, of course, the sovereign Lord is in control, though this does not seem to be the meaning here.

The scenario seems to be this: Satan's aim is to produce a masterpiece to match God's masterpiece, the Saviour of the world. However he is frustrated in his attempt, held back from bringing out the 'lawless one', Antichrist. Until the day when that restraint is removed, Satan must content himself with spreading the **spirit** of antichrist, lawlessness.

And when Antichrist comes, masterpiece it will certainly prove. Look how effective Satan's tool will be in deceiving mankind - *v 9 - 12.*

We are wise if we take careful notice of the methods he will use:
power ... signs ... wonders

Isn't that a familiar trio? Remember that Satan is out to deceive even the elect, if that were possible. How he must laugh when he sees us over-impressed by the miraculous. How he must fancy his chances of deceiving us with the lying wonders of Antichrist himself ...

Satan's tool? Yes, but God's too! God will harness Satan's masterpiece to prepare the world for Jesus' coming ...
- **God** allows people to be fooled because they refused to love the truth (v 10).
- **God** sends the spirit of delusion so they will fall for Antichrist's lies (v 11).
- **God's** purpose is to sort out those who in reality had 'pleasure in unrighteousness' from those who believed the truth (v 12).

And when God has finished using him, He will show how Satan's 'masterpiece' matches up to his own *(v 8)*...

Just a **breath** will consume him!
Just the **appearance** of Christ will destroy him!

We who look for Christ to come need not fear the lying wonders of Antichrist.

Read Matthew 24 v 21 - 35.

Standing fast   *2 Thessalonians 2 v 13 - 17*

What should be our reaction to Paul's teaching about Antichrist? *Read v 13 - 17.*

1. THANKSGIVING FOR SALVATION v 13, 14.

Thanksgiving, not fear! The appalling delusions of Antichrist give us fresh reason to thank God for the glorious certainty of salvation.

- **chosen from the beginning.** How secure then is the end, for our God does not change His mind! And He did not choose us merely to **convert** us, but to **save** us. Salvation in the New Testament means the whole work, from conversion right through to glory - God has chosen to see His people through to the end.
- **... through sanctification and faith.** These are the stepping stones to glory. Holy lives prove a faith that truly relies on the truth of God's Word. Both together prove that we are truly saved and on the path to glory.
- **... to obtain glory!** Let Antichrist do what he will; there can only be one destination for those God has called. Do not be afraid of temporary, though bitter, conflict - look up to the glory you will share in, that of Jesus Himself!

2. STANDING FAST TO THE TRUTH v 15

Thanksgiving for certain salvation does not lead to complacency. It is only **by** holding on to the truth that salvation is certain! Never let go of the truth that saved you in favour of a more attractive alternative. Only the truth that saved you in the beginning can save you to the end.

3. PRAYER FOR STRENGTH v 16, 17

We will certainly need it! Who has the strength and wisdom to hold out against the traps of the devil and the deceiving powers of Antichrist? But the One who has loved us has not left us to struggle on single-handedly ...

- **He has given us never-ending encouragement and hope (v 16).** We deserve none of it because of our failure and sin, but by His grace there is **always** encouragement and hope in Christ.
- **He gives the experience of encouragement and strength (v 17).** Paul prays that the **basis** for encouragement will result in everyday **experience** of it. That right now in our present circumstances He will give us courage and strength to **speak** and **act** for His glory. For that is God's purpose in comforting us. Not just to make us feel better, but to give us strength to serve Him better!

Do not forget this three-pronged formula for pressing on through difficulty and attack, of whatever kind. Which of the prongs are you most prone to neglect? How can you best keep balanced?

Read Paul's own testimony - *2 Corinthians 4 v 8 - 18.*

Faithful! 2 Thessalonians 3 v 1 - 5

The Thessalonian believers were not the only ones under attack! Just as they needed Paul's encouragement and instruction, so he needed their prayers in the tough time he was having at Corinth -

Read v 1, 2.

For Paul, praying for 'us' amounted to praying for the gospel. His longing was not for the gospel to gradually seep into the world, but to 'run' (literally) like a man in a race. The gospel cannot be glorified by keeping it hidden, but only by urgently proclaiming it far and wide.

Praying for 'us' meant something more specific too (v 2). For the gospel to 'run' through their ministry they needed prayer to be kept from enemy attack.

> How do our prayer requests compare with Paul's? Of course we have many different prayer needs, but is our great burden the same as his? And do many of our detailed requests for God's help have at their heart the spread and glorifying of the gospel?
>
> It is true that nothing is too small to bring to God, but it is also true that nothing is so great to plead for as the glorious gospel!

It is always important that we should never get so bogged down in our own troubles as to have no interest in others, but Paul does not labour the point. He turns back again to the needs of the Thessalonians -

Read v 3 - 5.

The Lord is faithful! (v 3)

There is a play on words here, from verse 2. The enemies' lack of faith accounts for their opposition; but the Lord's faithfulness is more than a match for it. Notice how it works in two ways; **strengthening us** to face the evil one's attacks, and **guarding us** from the harm he intends to do us. *Read John 17 v 15.*

You need to be faithful! (v 4)

Paul does not put it so bluntly, but that is the implication behind his confidence in them. Yes, the Lord would indeed strengthen and keep them, but only as they follow His commands. The Lord does not bless us through some kind of invisible injection; it is as **we** yield to His Word in loving obedience that we know **His** faithfulness.

The Lord make you faithful! (v 5)

Paul is only confident in them because he is confident in the Lord to keep them faithful! That is why he **prays** for them! The **love** of God is the great motivating force that will win our obedience. And the **endurance** of Christ is the great motivating force that we need to spur us on through persecution and trial.

Spend a while meditating on *Hebrews 12 v 1 - 4*, praying that God will direct you too into the meaning of His love and Christ's endurance to the death of the cross.

Busy workers not busybodies!   *2 Thessalonians 3 v 6 - 18*

Should church discipline be reserved for serious sexual sin or persistent drunkenness? Clearly not - *read v 6 - 15.*

Wouldn't a more gentle approach have been better, encouraging these lazy brothers to pull their weight? Yes, but the more gentle approach obviously had not worked - at least not for all! Now the issue was more serious, because they had rejected Paul's 'quiet word' in his first letter *(1 Thessalonians 4 v 11, 12).*

Discipline is appropriate **wherever the word of God is ignored**. Like parents disciplining their children, it is not always the offense itself that is serious, but the rebelling against authority. Always submit to God's authority, however small the issue might seem to be.

THE COMMAND - v 10 - 13

The issue was actually more important than we might think. It was threatening to disrupt the whole life of the church - as well as giving Christianity a bad name. Busybodies must stop being busy interfering and start being busy working.

But lest any should feel discouraged from being busy with good, constructive Christian work, Paul has a second command to balance the other! *v 13*

THE DISCIPLINE - v 6, 14, 15

It is vital not to be soft! Some kind souls were bound to take pity on these poor starving spongers, so Paul wisely speaks pretty firmly to the rest of the believers too (v 6). It is never kind to be soft, and let our fellow-believers get away with it. These people would soon start working when hunger began to bite - and the problem would be solved!

It is also vital not to be harsh. This discipline was not expulsion, but withdrawing of fellowship. And it was with loving reluctance, to their **brothers** (v 15). There was no question yet of thinking of them as unbelievers - that is the **last** thing to consider.

Compare *1 Corinthians 5 v 11 - 13* with *2 Corinthians 2 v 5 - 11.*

THE EXAMPLE - v 7 - 9

Exhortation is so much more powerful when it can be seen as well as heard! Paul had every right to expect the financial support of the Thessalonians, but had toiled into the early hours to avoid putting a burden on them. How ashamed these idle spongers should be!

Like Paul, we should always assess not only whether an action or choice would be **right**, but also how helpful an example it will leave for others.

Paul will not leave it on that rather difficult note; **peace** sums up his message and his longing for his dear friends - *read v 16 - 18.*

OUTLINE: 2 Thessalonians - stand fast!

🔑 '(may God) ... comfort your hearts and establish you in every good word and work' (2 v 17)

- ☞ Sum up each section in a short sentence or phrase (ideas below).
- ☞ Look for key words in each section (usually repeated).

SECTION	SUMMARY	KEYWORDS
1 v 1 - 5 v 6 - 12		
2 v 1 - 5 v 6 - 12 v 13 - 17		
3 v 1, 2 v 3 - 5 v 6 - 15 v 16 - 18		

stand fast ... pray for us ... rejoicing over their faith ... unbelievers will be deluded ... Jesus coming with justice ... the Lord of peace be with you ... Antichrist coming before Christ ... confidence in the Lord ... work quietly, discipline the disorderly

FACT - FILE : 1 Timothy

> **1 TIMOTHY**
>
> No other doctrine!

THE SITUATION

- Timothy was a spiritual son of Paul, who had worked faithfully alongside him on his second and third missionary journeys.
- Though reserved and somewhat timid, Timothy was a rare jewel so far as Paul was concerned. He could always trust Timothy to put the gospel first (Philippians 2 v 20 - 22).
- Later we find Timothy at Ephesus with the task of teaching and leading the church there. It is here that he receives his letters from Paul.
- Although the church at Ephesus had been established for some years, false teachers were spreading a mixture of errors, thus destabilising and threatening the church.

THE LETTER

- Written by Paul to Timothy around AD 65, after his first imprisonment at Rome. Paul is probably still in Macedonia (1 Timothy 1 v 3).
- Paul's aim is to refocus a rather hesitant Timothy on his calling and purpose. He must go on the offensive, combatting the spreading error by spreading the truth. To this end he must also establish right principles governing church leadership and give specific instructions for some of the disputed issues.
- After inspiring Timothy with his own example (chapter 1), Paul devotes the rest of the letter to instructions for public worship, appointing leaders, and for specific groups - all with an eye to combatting the false teaching they were being exposed to.
- See fuller outline at the end of the section.

If at all possible ...

Find time to read the letter through in one sitting, with this background in mind.

No other doctrine!   1 Timothy 1 v 1 - 7

Apostle to son! Straightaway Paul establishes the tone of his letter to his fellow-worker Timothy. It was going to be a mixture of apostolic authority and fatherly encouragement -

Read v 1, 2. See the kind of relationship Paul and Timothy enjoy, from *Philippians 2 v 19 - 23.*

Paul loses no time in going straight to the main point of his letter ...
'No other doctrine!'

Read v 3 - 7.

It was vital that Timothy should stick it out at Ephesus, standing up against the opposition. It was no mean task for timid Timothy to exert authority over these self-opinionated, self-appointed teachers of v 3, 6, 7, but for the truth's sake he must do it. Only one kind of doctrine must be taught at Ephesus - and only one kind of doctrine must be allowed in our own churches today ...

- *Teaching that produces 'godly edification' not disputes* (v 4)
  We must examine what teaching does for us. It may be stimulating and stirring, but if all it stirs up is controversy and argument then something is wrong. True teaching will certainly stir us up - it will stir up our **faith**, which as we exercise it, will **build us up in godliness** ('godly edification').

- *Teaching that promotes love, not pointless chatter* (v 5, 6)
  Is Timothy, in the interests of love, to permit a certain flexibility in what was taught at Ephesus? Are we to turn a blind eye to different strains of teaching that develop, for fear of disrupting fellowship? No! Paul means us to grasp that such reasoning is totally topsy-turvy. **Love** is the whole reason why Timothy is to clamp down on all other doctrine! Love can never thrive where false teaching is allowed to flourish. Love never comes from wrong doctrine but from ...
  - a pure heart; cleansed by the blood of Christ, renewed by the Spirit.
  - a good conscience; sensitive and obedient to the truth of God's Word, alert to sin.
  - genuine faith; not a play act, not a Sunday routine - but faith that works.

  And it was these basics that some had stopped teaching (v 6)! No wonder love was threatened! Meaningless debates over genealogies and speculative folklore around Old Testament characters was the kind of chatter that was displacing loving fellowship.

It would be worth spending a few moments thinking what is being produced by the teaching we receive (or give).

Only one kind of teaching - and one kind of teacher too (v 7). Not those who fancy themselves as teachers, nor those who have no real understanding of the truth, but people like Timothy and Paul ... *Read v 12.*

We should take James' words to heart - *James 3 v 1.*

Using the law lawfully   *1 Timothy 1 v 8 - 11, 18 - 20*

What is the main purpose of the Old Testament? To provide nice stories for Sunday School? For 'advanced' Christians with a bent for the ceremonial? To keep prophecy fanatics happily delving for years? Or to give these self-appointed teachers at Ephesus scope for vaunting their so-called expertise on names or ceremonial nicetes?

Would Paul lump you together with these teachers so far as your understanding of the 'law' (the whole of the Old Testament, broadly speaking) is concerned?

They don't know what they are talking about! (v 7)

What is the main purpose of the Old Testament? The answer is in *v 8 - 11*.

It is not to provide fascinating stories, but to **convict us of sin**. It is not for these sophisticated self-righteous teachers, but for **us who are sinners**. The law of God exposes us, it shows us how far short we fall of reaching God's standards ... it makes us painfully aware that v 9, 10 describe **ourselves**, not other 'wicked' people.

Notice how Paul slips in a phrase or two at the end of v 10 aimed at these false teachers; the law is just as relevant to them as to murderers or adulterers, if only they would see it.

But for Paul, to be reminded of the condemning finger of the law is to be reminded of the gospel (v 11)! The law not only points out our sin but points us to Christ. No wonder the true teaching of the law is to be jealously guarded; it was part of the gospel entrusted to Paul. Paul for one will never substitute his glorious message with the unprofitable irrelevances of the false teachers ...

And nor must Timothy. After Paul has got over the wonder of being entrusted with such a gospel (v 12 - 17, see tomorrow), he returns to his main point - that of urging Timothy to be faithful to such a gospel. *Read v 18 - 20.*

- **Timothy must be a good soldier ...** (v 18)
  Warfare may not be Timothy's scene, but that is what he was called to - and that is what he must engage in now. Like Timothy, we sometimes need to be re-'charged' to pick up our weapons again and fight the only good warfare there can be ... the battle for the truth.

- **... and a good sailor** (v 19)
  That means   **going in the right direction** - holding onto the **faith** (i.e the truth).
           by keeping firm hold of the rudder - being steered by the testimony of our **conscience** to the truth.
  Abandon these and shipwreck is inevitable. Our faith is on the rocks, our hope of eternal life dashed.

There are many shipwrecks for us all to see (v 20). Be warned by them; do not join them on the rocks. *Read 2 Timothy 2 v 17 - 19,* and Timothy's aim - to bring them back - *v 23 - 26.*

Grace abounding to the chief of sinners *1 Timothy 1 v 12 - 17*

Call these verses a diversion if you like, but it is a glorious one! And relevant too, because Paul wants Timothy to be bursting with gratitude at God's amazing grace, just as he was himself. For then Timothy will cling like a limpet to his glorious gospel and be as eager as a beaver to fulfil his commission ...

Read v 12 - 17.

1. EXCEEDING GRACE IN SAVING HIM (v 13 - 16)

- **Exceeding sinner.** The sovereign Lord loves to call the most unlikely candidates. Paul was not seeking Christ - he was seeking to kill all Christ's followers! He was bitterly and violently anti-Christ, the 'chief of sinners'. (Paul is not trying to excuse himself in v 13; he is just explaining how it was possible that even the chief of sinners could ever be saved. Mercy, praise God, was possible because he had not deliberately sinned against the Holy Spirit with clear belief in Jesus as God's Son.)

- **Exceeding grace.** Where sin abounded, grace super-abounded (v 14)! There is no other explanation for our salvation; sheer mercy in return for sheer sin. Yet there was one other reason why God had shown mercy to Paul - so that no-one throughout history should despair (v 16)! Paul was to be a pattern - as if he had 'mercy for the chief of sinners' written all over him - for the worst sinner to take hope from. Is that you ...?

2. EXCEEDING GRACE IN COMMISSIONING HIM (v 12)

Paul would have been more than happy to have scraped into the kingdom, as it were, living his Christian life in disgrace as the wretch who had tormented so many believers. But God's exceeding grace had different plans! The chief of sinners was to be the chief of apostles! The fanatic who was so zealous to persecute was 'counted faithful' to preach (v 12)! Not for anything he had done - how could that be! - but because God's grace was going to **make** him trustworthy.

Amazing grace indeed; yet who could be better suited to tell the whole world that it was for **sinners** that Christ came to die? Paul has long passed to glory, but in a sense his commission lives on. While only sinners **commissioned** by exceeding grace can dare to **preach**, can any sinner **saved** by amazing grace keep the glorious message to himself...?

Read Acts 26 v 9 - 18; Luke 24 v 46 - 48.

Paul has done his best - but how can the infinite glory of God's mercy be fully described? He can only resort to doxology, and so should we - *read v 17.*

Pray for all!   *1 Timothy 2 v 1 - 7*

So how is Timothy to combat these false teachers? What specifics need to be insisted upon? Top of Paul's list is that **this gospel is for everyone**. The church at Ephesus was not to focus solely on Jews or any other exclusive group (as perhaps the false teachers suggested), but on all kinds of people everywhere!

With that in mind *read v 1 - 7* a few times. (This section is often misunderstood, but reading it through together helps us see its main meaning, and guard against wrongly interpreting individual verses - a basic principle for Bible-reading!) To summarise;
- pray for all (groups of) people (including kings, prime ministers etc), because ...
- salvation is for all (groups of) people (as there is only this one way of salvation), so that...
- Paul is called to preach to all (groups of) people (Gentiles as well as Jews)

With that structure in place we can afford to zoom in on some of the detail;

❏ **Pray for all people; v 1 - 3**
We all know how easy it is to get into a rut in praying 'for the royal family and all in authority'! Perhaps our prayers have been lacking both the **rich variety** and **urgent purpose** intended by these verses. Specific requests for known needs combine with general prayer for continual needs. Calling on God to intervene in lives joins with thanksgiving (v 1); always with that great goal in view, for 'all men' to be saved. And 'all men' does not mean **solely** those in power! What about the unreached groups of Muslims, or young people, or single parents or ...? There are so many specific situations to consider when we really start praying for **all** categories. And verse 2 is not for a rather self-centred cosy existence; stable government is crucial for the advance of the gospel!

❏ **Because salvation is for all people; v 4 - 6**
'All' has many different uses in the Bible, so the context must decide. Kings and beggars, Jews and Gentiles, Hindus and Buddhists, Fascists and Communists, from New York to Tokyo, can only come one way to God. There is only one Mediator who stands between God and sinners - Jesus Christ. There is no other way of salvation! And God's concern does not miss out on any type of person; His gospel is gloriously relevant to all. Before grumbling inwardly that Christ did not pay the ransom for every individual sinner, ought we not to check that our own love for souls is as broad as His? That our prayers and evangelistic endeavours are not in fact limited to 'nice', religiously-minded, middle-class whites? *Matthew 4 v 13 - 17.*

❏ **So that Paul is called to preach to all people; v 7**
Especially the Gentiles! Those for whom there had been no hope, no way to God! Despised and dismissed by those (Jews) in the secret. If our **prayers** reach out to all men, will not our **message** reach out too, even to those groups that seem so alien to us ...?
Read Paul's policy; *1 Corinthians 9 v 20 - 23, 26, 27.*

The woman's place ...   *1 Timothy 2 v 8 - 15*

So who is to lead public prayer as in v 1 - 7? Not just 'people in general', but the men in particular rather than the women. *Read v 8* and note the contrast with v 9.

Some may feel uncomfortable and wish this section had been missed out of the Bible. But is that because we have been unconsciously moulded by the world's opinions rather than allowing our views to be transformed by the Word of God? Try to shed any preconceived ideas for a moment and listen to what God says;

Read v 9 - 15.

TWO OUTFITS
v 9, 10

Just as men should prepare themselves for prayer (by dealing with wrong attitudes to fellow-believers, v 8), so should the women see they are 'dressed' attractively.
Attractively, that is, to God. How totally out of place to entertain any thoughts of impressing other women, or pulling men, when we are preparing to bow in humble worship of our glorious God!
Notice the two kinds of 'outfit' that will give real pleasure to God. Will that affect the way you dress? The way you live?

TWO ROLES
v 11, 12

1. Learn. 2. Submit. And just in case we have missed the point, Paul puts it other way round in v 12. 1. Don't teach men. 2. Don't rule over men. In other words women are to be women and not men. They are not to fight against what God has made them and the role He has given them.
Never think that God holds some kind of grudge against the women, who after all He Himself has made! It is we, not He, who underrate women if we despise the vital roles He has given them ...

TWO REASONS
v 13, 14

It is wise to read these verses before crying out 'But times have changed!' It is as if Paul saw it coming! Yes, of course certain Bible **customs** have changed (do you wash your brother's feet?), but Bible **principles** have not. Since Adam was made a man and Eve a woman, men have not ceased being men, nor women given up their womanhood. So one reason is *God made us like this.* But did you notice a second, in v 14? *Look what happened when woman played the man!* Is it not enough for us that we have messed up creation by getting our roles wrong ... or will we insist on wrecking the church too?

TWO REPONSI- BILITES
v 15

Some descendants of Eve may still be fighting against feelings of being treated as a spare part. Sadly in some churches men may still undervalue women, but God does not - see v 15! What greater responsibility could there be? What greater honour? What greater life-work? And what greater privilege and fulfilment than to bring children up in the fear of the Lord? Yes, she must bear the curse of painful childbirth because of Eve's disobedience, but her 'salvation' will be to know the indescribable joy of seeing her children come to salvation. But she must never forget her other great responsibility. For the joys of Christian motherhood are known only by a **continuing** relationship with the Lord ...

Read 1 Peter 3 v 1 - 7.

Qualified overseers   *1 Timothy 3 v 1 - 7*

The second 'faithful saying' on which Paul puts his stamp of approval. And that means we are not free to disagree with him, or even to relegate it to a position of minor importance ...

Read v 1 - 7.

Do not frown on aspirations to such a great work. Encourage those who want to be a 'bishop' (overseer, elder, pastor)! So long as ...
(1) the motives are right. To get to the top is, in Jesus' eyes, to go for the **humblest** not the **highest** position ...
(2) it is seen as a great **'work'** (v 1). Overseers do just what their name says! They 'watch over' the souls and lives of fellow-believers on behalf of Jesus Himself. And that means hard labour; *agonising in prayer ... toiling at teaching ... pleading for obedience ... bleeding over disobedience ...*

I understand all that. And I know God is calling me to this work ...

Wonderful! So out he goes into the ministry. Or in he goes into the eldership of the church...? That is just how Christ's church becomes infested with the kind of self-appointed false teachers that were plaguing these believers! And that is why Paul gives Timothy - and us - the rather searching tests of v 2 - 7 ...

- *Is he blameless?* The first one on the list may be intended as a heading for all of v 2 - 6. Above reproach in all those areas - and all others - so that no-one can justly point a despising finger and say *'What him, an overseer, with a temper like that ... with his extravagant spending habits ... but didn't you know that he ... ?!'*
- *Is he able to teach?* (v 2) In Christ's church leading means teaching. Overseeing is always bringing people under God's Word. The great goal is for all under their care to lead lives ever closer to the teaching of the Bible. Overseers just cannot do their job if they do not have the gift to teach (and the blank looks will soon give it away).
- *Is he able to rule?* (v 4, 5) The family is the best place to test this one (though if he is not married other situations may be helpful - such as Sunday School class). If his children (or wife) run rings round him then so will the church. Yet he wins obedience by winning respect, not by beating into cowed submission.
- *Is he a novice?* (v 6) How many promising young men are wrecked by being thrust into a position of such influence before they have learnt how to handle their pride? You can't get much worse condemnation than that which is shared by the devil himself ...
- *Is he respected outside?* Blameless in the church's eyes (v 1 - 6) and blameless in the world's estimation (v 7). He may be laughed at for his faith, laughed at for his witness, but do they have to admit that he lives by what he says? Or will the devil be laughing when he is appointed overseer, because he knows the man will bring his double standards into the church?

The pressure may be on to put Doug into the ministry, or to appoint Mr Jones as elder. But be sure of this; **God** has not called him if he falls short of these qualifications. We appoint him at our peril, his peril, the church's peril - and in rebellion against the Word of Christ.

Read Acts 20 v 17 - 35. (Notice Paul's Example, Testimony, Warning to these elders.)

Serving deacons   *1 Timothy 3 v 8 - 16*

Deacons are not second-rate, not-so-spiritual elders; they have different responsibilities. While elders/overseers/pastors **rule** and **teach**, deacons **serve** in a practical sphere.

Read v 8 - 12, contrasting the kind of person a deacon is to be, with the five points noted yesterday.

- **Some characteristics are different.** Deacons have no need to be teachers, for example - but they must still hold on to the faith, conscientiously living to please God in everything (v 9).

- **Many are the same.** There is no relaxation of standards for deacons! The same care must be taken in appointing them, as they are public ministers of the church of Jesus Christ.

Just as v 1 serves as an encouragement to would-be overseers, so *v 13* spurs deacons on. Serving God faithfully always carries its rewards. You might not think that performing the practical tasks of a deacon, for example, would do much for your spiritual progress, but God knows better! Honour ... assurance ... bold testimony - these are the fruits of devoted service to God.

See how that worked out in the life of Stephen; *Acts 6 v 1 - 10.*

Now read v 14 - 16.

Why are all these instructions so important? Why couldn't they have waited till Paul came himself?

- **Because it is the church of the living God (v 15).** It is not Mr So-and-so's church (for then you might excuse it being rather a shambles), but the church of God Himself. His church is to be 'the pillar and ground of **truth**', not the seed bed of all kinds of error! And that means godly and strong leadership, as a matter of urgency.

- **Because it is the church of the living Jesus (v 16). He** is the mystery of godliness! The mystery of 'God with us', the secret which He lets us into when we come to know Christ. It is the church of the once-manifested-in-the-flesh-but-now-reigning-in-glory Lord. The One whom angels and God testified to be the Son of God, the One who is preached and believed on as Saviour and Lord. He, too, is watching to see if we have captured anything of His grandeur and glory in our churches ...

Falling from faith   *1 Timothy 4 v 1 - 5*

There is another reason why the church at Ephesus urgently needed the right leaders to watch over and carefully teach the believers ...

Apostasy! Falling away from the faith! *Read v 1 - 5.*

They had been specifically warned of this (e.g Acts 20 v 28 - 31, to the Ephesian elders a few years earlier), and the seeds were already being sown. The 'latter times' when people would be drawn away from the faith were almost upon them.

There will always be people professing faith in Christ who after a while lose interest or find the going too tough. But Paul is warning of a particular danger - a time when **false teaching** will be very successful in deceiving the unsuspecting. Just as the Ephesians were to be prepared for such a period in the 1st and 2nd centuries, so must we be ready for the great apostasy just before the second coming of Christ.

What are the marks of these false teachers?

1. Lies. Paul does not mince words. Anything that deviates from the truth is simply lies. It is not a valid alternative, not just another, equally acceptable theology, but devilish lies. and 'devilish' is not too strong a word, because any teaching that is false originates not from God but Satan (v 1).

So why are these lies so successful? Because they do not look like lies. The arguments are so plausible and so attractive. Often they play on our emotions and entice us away from the Word of God. The only way to be safe is to cling like a limpet to the truth that saved you, the rock of the Bible.

2. Hypocrisy. We like to imagine that they are all genuine - wrong, but sincere. Again, Paul is blunt, and surprisingly sweeping. These are people who have refused to listen to their conscience - and overexposed consciences just don't work the same. Now they can piously talk people into believing their teaching, while cynically pursuing a self-centred, even immoral life.

What are the errors of these false teachers?

Somewhat minor you might think from v 3 - 5! Why ever is Paul so concerned over such insignificant error? From his alarmed tones you would have imagined the great central truths of salvation were under attack!

They were. As soon as Christianity becomes a matter of **our own efforts** it will lead many to deserting their **faith in Christ**. To insist on abstention from marriage or from certain foods is to insist on a works religion. Such teaching is lethal.

Perhaps the devil would never deceive you by going straight for the fundamentals, but he can just as surely ruin souls by starting with what seems so innocent, even helpful ...

Jude gives forceful teaching on facing dangerous times. Read his short letter.

A profitable exercise *1 Timothy 4 v 6 - 10*

To face up to the false teachers and dangers of v 1 - 5, Timothy needed all the encouragement he could get. Here it is! Marks of a good servant of Jesus Christ to spur Timothy - and us - onwards.

Read v 6 - 10.

INSTRUCT
v 6

Number one priority for a good pastor. Teaching truth is the only way of combatting error, and the only way of promoting growth. And notice what happens as the minister feeds others - he is 'nourished' himself! ('brought up', NIV) Not by going after new, exciting ideas, but sticking faithfully to the old, precious truths.

REJECT
v 7

'Be positive' urge some people. Yes, but not always. The good minister will drive out the bad as well as driving home the good. And that is not so easy because it means running the risk of offending Christian friends who are less choosy.

EXERCISE
v 8, 9

Physically if and when you can. But spiritually as an absolute priority. Our goal is not to be fit enough to run five miles, but to be fit to serve the Lord. And that means one thing - godliness. We are no good if we have no godliness. Notice the two great advantages godliness has over physical fitness:
- it profits for **all things**. Some people become fanatical over getting fit - but it only benefits them in one small area of life! But focus on godliness and your whole life is enriched.
- it profits for **all time**. Unlike physical fitness the effects do not wear off. Godliness is never lost, it always accumulates. And the benefits last for all eternity!

But do stop to consider the implications of the word 'exercise'. Godliness does not drop down from the skies. Exercise means 'diet', self-discipline, time, and of course ...

LABOUR
v 10

Godliness never comes easily. Neither in ourselves nor as we teach others. But think of the effort you are prepared to put into your exams, or your job. Think of the years of training you are happy to do to pursue your chosen career. Is not your career in godliness worth far more labour than that?

SUFFER
v 10

Satan hates godliness. The world hates godliness. Be godly and suffer for it - but you will never regret it. And all along you will have a God to ...

TRUST
v 10

The God who sent Jesus to be Saviour of the world, who welcomes sinners everywhere to be reconciled through Him. Can we not rest in this kind, generous God who cares so deeply for all? And can we not rest in His **special** saving love in dying for all who come to put their faith in Him?

Only by trusting God will we become godly, and only by becoming godly will we become good servants of Jesus Christ.

Read Paul's own example as a good minister; *2 Corinthians 6 v 1 - 11.*

All-round minister   *1 Timothy 4 v 11 - 16*

It is easy to become unbalanced in serving God - especially when you are younger, like Timothy. Pehaps you really get a burden for one particular thing, and go for it with a vengeance, but at the same time the dust is gathering on other areas.

There are two main sides to the ministry, both of which split into many other concerns;

'Take heed to YOURSELF and to the DOCTRINE' (v 16)   *Read v 11 - 16.*

YOURSELF

We can easily imagine that Timothy was rather conscious of his youth (probably in his 30's), and anxious about exerting authority over older Christians (v 12). But he must see himself as God's appointed minister; his authority comes from his position, not his age. (And, of course, Paul has it in mind that the whole church would be seeing this letter!) Still, there is another important side to it; the best way to lead is not by command but example ...

- **in word.** He must watch how he speaks out of the pulpit - because others will!
- **in conduct.** If his life does not match up to his teaching then nor will his hearers'.
- **in love.** Anything done without love would have been better not done at all ...
- **in spirit.** Not only love, but willingness, gratitude, enthusiasm, humility ...
- **in faith.** Trusting in trial, expecting answers to prayer, bold in moving forward with God.
- **in purity.** Never a suspicion of over-friendliness, never a straying look.

A relevant test for us all!
- In which of these areas are we a good / indifferent / poor example?
- What therefore needs to change? How?

DOCTRINE

That is, the whole of the teaching ministry (v 13). Timothy must not be tempted to concentrate on the parts that come easier to him (perhaps **reading** the scriptures and teaching **doctrine**), but include the warnings and reproofs, commands and encouragements that are all part of **exhortation.**

Remember it is not up to us to choose whether to use the gifts that God has given us! He gave them not for our own amusement, but for the building up of His church (v 14). ***Read Ephesians 4 v 7 - 16.***

Meditate ... give yourself entirely ... take heed ... continue' (v 15, 16). That is how seriously Timothy is to take both areas of his ministry. He is to be wrapped up in it, constantly watching out for anything that is beginning to slip. Then his progress will be obvious for all to see.

For it is not **beginning** a Christian life that guarantees our salvation, but **continuing** to the end. *'He that endures to the end shall be saved'* (Matthew 10 v 22)
Read Philippians 2 v 12, 13.

Widows in need *1 Timothy 5 v 1 - 8*

Having dealt with Timothy's ministry in general, Paul gets down to some detail. How is the minister to treat individual groups?

Read v 1, 2.

Never as the underdog! The church is no business organisation, but a family. Everyone is to be treated as an individual with particular needs - and always as **at least** an equal!

- **older men.** Never harshly or insensitively, but always with the respect due to a father.
- **younger men.** The easiest group to exert superiority over, but no - 'as **brothers**'
- **older women.** With the tenderness and love shown to mothers.
- **younger women.** This needs special wisdom. They are sisters so deserve affection, yet combined with a dignity that avoids all danger of impurity.

Now for the delicate issue of financial support for groups in particular need! Unlike the harsh world around, God's people are to care for one another very practically, and yet the church is not to be a soft touch.

What are the principles Timothy is to apply? *Read v 3 - 8.*

1. Look after your own family (v 4, 8). Notice how Paul emphasises it - positively in v 4 and negatively (very!) in v 8. It is never 'good and acceptable' to God to be so busy serving in the church to have no time to serve in the home. That is where piety must begin. So far as God is concerned it is no Christianity at all that has little time for old people when they are dependent. Putting them in an old peoples' home (though **sometimes** the most caring option) is too often a callous and ungrateful slap in the face for all the care and attention so unstintingly given when we were the dependent ones.

2. Support widows who really are widows. (v 3, 5 - 7). Verse 5 defines what that means:
- widows left alone with no family to support them.
- widows who put their trust in God.

The church is not there to fund those whose affections are firmly rooted in the pleasure this world has to offer. That is like giving money to dead people because their life is only really a living death (v 6). But to support dear believing widows who have nothing left but their God is the privilege of God's family.

Perhaps these verses have implications for Christians giving to those in need ...

Stick to these principles and the world cannot fairly point a finger (v 7). But fail to care for those God has given us to care for and it will be God's finger as well as the world's that is pointing at us ...

Because **He** cares especially for widows if we will not: e.g *Psalm 146 v 9; Exodus 22 v 22, 23; Luke 7 v 11 - 17.*

Widows at work *1 Timothy 5 v 9 - 16*

This section presents us with a problem. Timothy would have known just what Paul was referring to, but for us looking on 2,000 years later, it is impossible to be sure. Was the 'number' or 'list' of widows in v 9 simply the widows Paul has already described - or was it a particular group set apart for prayer and work in the church? Either way the careful qualifications seem to suggest that these were widows with special responsibilities and commitment to the Lord's work;

Read v 9 - 16.

If we cannot be sure of the precise meaning of scripture, it is safest to home in on the principles that come out of it;

1. Older widows are valuable in the church.

Usually they have plenty of that commodity which those of us who are younger tend to be short of - time! And when you couple that with the wisdom, maturity and grace that comes from a life of serving the Lord, then you have a valuable combination indeed! And it is not to be wasted; idleness, gossip and interfering do not become respectable with old age. They are as much sins for older widows as they are for younger (v 13).

Of course prayer is the most valuable of all work for widows (v 5), but not the **only** work! Older people often become discouraged because they feel there is little else they can do, but is that because their gifts are undervalued? We should greatly value them, use them, encourage them. And pray for them as they so faithfully pray for us.

Read Luke 2 v 36 - 38 - an active widow!

2. Younger widows should not bear unnatural pressure.

However willing they are to commit themselves to the Lord's work, their first calling as younger women is to marry and bear children. If they were to make this 'widow's vow' to serve the Lord, the pressure to break it when they meet that lovely man would simply be too great (this seems to be the meaning of v 11, 12). Besides, younger women have more available energy and are far more likely to fall into the sin of gossipy idleness, their visiting becoming a definite hazard to church life rather than a means of Christian encouragement (v 13).

Paul speaks with a decisiveness that seems to come from unhappy experience when he excludes these younger widows from the 'number' and advises them to find a husband! (v 14, 15). Perhaps some had already not only broken this 'widow's vow' to Christ, but deserted the faith altogether, to the disgrace of the church and glee of the enemy.

Whether older or younger, married or widowed, God has a place for every one of His people in His church. Have you found that place? Or are you sitting by, watching others using their energy for the Lord's work and the Lord's glory?

Read Romans 14 v 7, 8.

Back to elders   *1 Timothy 5 v 17 - 25*

The question of finance brings Paul back to the topic of elders; *Read v 17 - 25.*

DOUBLE HONOUR v 17 - 19.

By 'double' honour, Paul does not restrict himself to two reasons for honouring elders! Let's take to heart **all** the ideas that are jostling together in these verses:
> Honour the elders for their God-given position of authority! (v 17)
> Honour good elders for the wise way they lead! (v 17)
> Honour elders who give everything they have to teach you the Word of God! (v 17)
> Honour elders by supporting them financially as they are working for your souls! (v 18)
> Honour elders by refusing to listen to rumours or unsupported negative comments! (v 19)

Does that make quintuple honour?! Certainly it makes a lot more than they are commonly given ...

Paul could have done with a bit more honour from the Corinthians! *Read 1 Corinthians 9 v 3 - 18.*

DOUBLE DISCIPLINE v 20, 21.

The loyalty of v 19 must never mean that elders get away with anything they like! Rather the opposite - because our loyalty to the church and to Jesus Christ must come before solidarity for the elders. Just because they are highly respected and loved in the church does not mean discipline gets swept under the carpet. In fact it works exactly the other way about! Public servants of the church are to be disciplined publicly, so that others see and tremble, and the purity of the church is preserved. *(James 3 v 1)*

And lest fellow leaders should be tempted to be lenient on their dear brother, their close friend, their relative, they should remember that the impartial Judge of all is looking over their shoulder. V 21 is pretty strong, but that is because favoritism would result in wrecking all Timothy's efforts to deal with the false teachers and to establish the Ephesian church.

DOUBLE CARE v 22- 25.

The buck does not always stop at the sinning leader! Was it a rushed appointment? A popular choice? Scant attention to chapter 3? Then someone else shares the blame for that sin. Timothy must keep himself 'pure' by taking great care over appointing elders. (And, by the way Timothy, be conscientious over that but not over-conscientious about drinking wine for the sake of your health. The work must not suffer for a neutral issue!)

And when elders are appointed do not go by the WYSIWYG principle! (For those still resisting the computer age: **W**hat **Y**ou **S**ee (on the screen) **I**s **W**hat **Y**ou **G**et (on the printout.)) A casual glance at a man's life is not enough; some men's sins are as clear as daylight, for others What You Get will be nasty surprises if you go by What You See (v 24). And it works the other way too; a few discreet enquiries will soon bring to the surface the quiet but committed zeal of some you almost forgot to consider! (v 25)

Doctrine leading to godliness   *1 Timothy 6 v 1 - 6*

One last group that needs special attention, to go along with the others in chapter 5;

Read v 1, 2.

If you work for a Christian boss there are a couple of things to keep in mind:
- He is your boss. You are one in Christ but you are not equals at work. Respect is due - even over unpopular decisions!
- He is a Christian. So you have an added incentive to work well. An opportunity to serve your brother.

That all sounds obvious, but human nature being what it is, our attitudes can be just the opposite of these! Tension and resentment builds up because we hate an equal having authority over us. It is easy to imagine that was quite a problem for a **slave**; *'How can he call me his brother and still keep me in slavery!'*

Whether or not your boss is a Christian, never forget the world is keeping close tabs on you (v 1). Somehow unbelievers have an acute sense of how Christians ought not to behave!

Paul's teaching has not been vague, general ideals, but practical instructions that bite. And with one aim in view - **godliness**. A far cry from the teaching of those we have already met (chapter 1 v 3 - 7) - *read v 3 - 6.*

- **different words** (contrast v 3 and 4). Not the wholesome health-giving words of Jesus Christ Himself. They could not agree to this kind of teaching, but insisted on wranglings over obscure meanings, using words as weapons to win arguments rather than as truth to win souls.
- **different results.** Health-giving words not surprisingly give health! In other words **godliness** (v 3). But if these are rejected what else can be expected than the sickness of v 4?
  Stop for a moment and examine the words you use. Your teaching, your conversation. Healthy? Life-giving? Promoting godliness? Or more likely to promote the ugly fruits of envy, dispute, insult, distrust?
- **different motives.** Those who teach wholesome words only want godliness. They have no ulterior motives. To be godly is to be rich, both for themselves and their hearers (v 6). But godliness is a totally foreign idea to the others. Their one goal in religion is to promote themselves, to gain power and influence, success and wealth (v 5).
- **different characters.** V 5 sums it up. These people are not **Christians**. Their minds are depraved and their hearts destitute. They are proud of themselves but ignorant of the truth (v 4). Even if we have begun to get friendly with them we must recognise they are dangerous. Have nothing to do with them! Get right away from them! (v 5)

Peter is not exaggerating when he describes similar characters so graphically in *2 Peter 2*. Don't be deceived.

Handling our finances   *1 Timothy 6 v 7 - 10, 17 - 19.*

Ambition! Good or bad? I suppose the answer depends on who it is for and what it is aimed at.
Contentment! Good or bad? Again, doesn't it all depend...?

Unfortunately most of us have got it the wrong way round. Ambitious for wealth, pleasure and fulfilment, but content with our 'godliness'. Ambitious for ourselves, but content with our efforts for God. Paul has some timely advice for us;

FOR THE WOULD-BE-RICH *read v 6 - 10.*

- **Be content!** Job had got this right. So Paul borrows v 7 from this man who certainly knew what he was talking about. *Read Job 1 v 14 - 21.*
  Job had done his sums properly. We tend to think of our comforts - and even luxuries - as if we had a right to them. We count it an injustice if we cannot afford to run a car or own a washing machine! But Job knew there was no injustice even when we lose everything. None of his vast possessions were his when he was born, none would be his after he died. It was all on loan from God. So will you be content to let the wise, kind God decide how much is best for you to 'borrow' for a while?

- **Be warned!** The love of money is Satan's trap. And a highly successful and lethal one at that. For at least two reasons;
  - Indulge it and you will always want more. Desire for money is never satisfied.
  - Indulge it and you will indulge in anything. Take v 9, 10 very seriously. Give in to those 'harmless' expensive tastes and there is no telling what 'harmful lusts' will close their grip on you. There is a chilling progression in v 9. Desire ... fall ... drown.

FOR THE ALREADY-RICH *read v 17 - 19.*

There is nothing wrong with being rich ... but it needs incredibly careful handling! Two vital keys:

- **Trust in God!** Verse 17 is a favorite one to quote - but it is nearly always lifted out of context. Paul is not teaching that God gives us everything to richly enjoy - he is simply assuming it! Of course it is true, but the real point is this: **trust the God who gives!** Take your eyes off the good gifts and fix them firmly on the good God! The only safe way to enjoy the riches is to love God.

- **Invest in giving!** Copy God. *'Freely you have received, freely give.'* And you will find something amazing happens - the more richly you give, the richer you become! Not necessarily in increased income - but that has now become of minor interest anyway. No, you have learned the priceless secret that giving temporal riches reaps eternal dividends. Giving away what is ours for a while pays into our own account benefits that will be ours for ever!
  In what ways is that true? What are the lasting benefits mentioned in *2 Corinthians 9 v 6 - 15*?

O Timothy!   *1 Timothy 6 v 11 - 21*

Riches are to hold no attraction for Timothy. He is a 'man of God' not a man of the world. He is not even to hang around in the danger zone but run from the first hint of a fatal attraction for money. But it is not all negative ...

Read v 11 - 21.

Pursue! Fight! Lay hold! (v 11, 12)

Christians are always to be on the offensive, always pressing forwards, always attacking. The way to reject the devil's enticements to pursue riches is to pursue the riches of v 11 for all we are worth.
- Stop to consider each of those treasures. How much pursuing are you actually doing?
- *'Fight the good fight of faith'* and *'Lay hold of eternal life'* are rousing phrases, but think through what they mean in practice.

Paul always seems to be urging Timothy to action! But his exhortations are backed up with **motivations** to help Timothy - and us - to respond.
- *God is watching - and He is the One who gives life* (v 13). We owe Him our life and He watches over our life.
- *Christ is watching - and He never flinched in the face of death* (v 13). Paul can encourage Timothy because he had already made a good, bold confession of Jesus - just as Jesus Himself had (v 12). Surely now he will not give way to fear ...
- *Christ is coming - will He find us blameless?* (v 14). Will we be ashamed then because we are ashamed now? It will be too late then to keep His commands. All pursuing, all fighting, all witnessing will be over then.
- *God will reveal Christ - this glorious sovereign God!* (v 15, 16). Every phrase underlines the supremacy and glory of our God. Will we not submit to the commands of the King of kings? Meditate for a while on these two verses and surely any fear of man will turn into adoring reverence for your God. Then you will gladly obey ...

O Timothy, guard ...! (v 20, 21)

It has a familiar ring by now, but that is because Paul is burdened! He has seen fellow-labourers wrecked because they gave in to the pressures.
Demas was one (although this may have been later) - *2 Timothy 4 v 10.*

Do you share Paul's burden? Pray for pastors that they will remain faithful to the Word of God! Pray for your own church, that it will jealously guard the truth entrusted to it. Pray for yourself, that you will not be enticed away from the faith that saved you.

Read 2 Timothy 4 v 1 - 8.

OUTLINE: 1 Timothy - no other doctrine

'O Timothy! Guard what was committed to your trust ...' (6 v 20)

- Sum up each section in a short sentence or phrase (ideas below).
- Look for key words in each section (usually repeated).

SECTION	SUMMARY	KEYWORDS
1 v 1-11 v 12-20		
2 v 1-7 v 8-15		
3 v 1-7 v 8-13 v 14-16		
4 v 1-5 v 6-16		
5 v 1-16 v 17-25		
6 v 1, 2 v 3-10 v 11-16 v 17-19 v 20, 21		

godly exercise, godly example ... be content! ... qualities of overseers ... pray for all men ... no other doctrine! ... right use of riches ... O Timothy, keep! ... honour masters ... qualities of deacons ... modest, submissive women ... He counted me faithful! ... right conduct in God's church ... honour widows ... apostasy coming ... pursue! fight! keep! ... honour elders

FACT - FILE : 2 Timothy

> **2 TIMOTHY**
>
> Fight on!

THE SITUATION

- ☞ Refer back to FACTFILE on 1 Timothy.
- ☞ A year or two later, Timothy is probably still in Ephesus, where error is still flourishing and persecution has set in.

THE LETTER

- ☞ Paul's situation has changed dramatically. No longer free to travel and preach the gospel, he is again in prison in Rome, awaiting a death that now seems certain. The date is around AD 65 - this is probably the last of Paul's New Testament letters.
- ☞ Paul's purpose is similar to that of his first letter. Yet, in view of his own pending death, the tone is perhaps more urgent, and there is more personal encouragement for Timothy. He must carry on the battle, throwing himself into preaching sound doctrine, whatever persecution and hardship that would involve.
- ☞ One theme fills the whole letter. Paul reasons and urges and commands Timothy to preach on to the end, like he himself has, expecting it to be tough, expecting opposition from evil men.
- ☞ See fuller outline at the end of the section.

If at all possible ...

Find time to read the letter through in one sitting, with this background in mind.

Remember and press on　　　　　　　　　　　　　　　　　　　*2 Timothy 1 v 1 - 7*

There are a lot more Timothys around than Pauls! Naturally on the timid side, hesitant, put off by painful experiences ... most of us find it easier to identify with such a figure than with the seemingly invincible apostle.

Yet Paul is amazingly good at understanding how we lesser mortals feel - surely because in fact he has faced just the same struggles himself! Notice how by hints, reassurances and exhortations he reminds Timothy of just what he needs to get him on his feet again - *read v 1 - 7.*

- *Remember the business we are about - v 1.* Don't we too often lose sight of the life-and-death-ness of it all? It is not a mere hobby you can drop if it becomes too much of a hassle; it is not even a favourite topic you can keep quiet about when it receives a hostile reception. If you want to have any **hope of real life, eternal life**, for yourself and fellow human beings, then don't duck out of the battle!

- *Remember how much I care about you - v 2 - 4.* 'I am right there with you Timothy, my dear son! You are constantly in my prayers and I cannot tell you how much I long to see you again and turn those tears at our last parting into joy.' Imagine how much that would have meant to Timothy ... imagine how much **your** faithful prayers and love could mean to believers who perhaps are floundering ...

- *Remember the reality of your faith - v 5.* Tempted to give up? To chuck it all in? But if you do that it means there must have been no truth in it at the beginning; either because Christianity is all a hoax or because your own conversion experience was phoney. If you were genuinely born again you simply cannot be unborn!
  For Timothy there was no doubt; the foundations of his faith were solid - he knew for sure his faith was not something he could simply give up on.

- *Remember the gift God gave you - v 6, 7.* Notice how Paul links gifts with faith. Just as a Christian cannot throw away his faith, so he cannot opt to throw away his gifts. Jesus' parable makes it clear that a Christian who buries his gifts is no Christian at all - *Read Matthew 25 v 14 - 30.*
  No, Timothy (and all of us who are Christians) must fan into flames the embers of his neglected gifts. Neither fear nor timidity must stop us, for along with the gift God provides power, love and clear thinking to put the gift into action. Think through how each of those three qualities are so vital as we seek to serve the Lord with the particular gifts He has given each of His people.

Perhaps you were not feeling particularly timid - but was it lazy, or just drifting along? Use the four reminders to stir up the gifts God has given you, to serve Him with renewed vigour and love.

Shame or suffering? *2 Timothy 1 v 8 - 12*

Ashamed of Jesus? Most of us recoil from the thought; the last person we have any reason to be ashamed of is our glorious Saviour! And yet which of us has never been embarrassed to be seen with Christians ... ducked out from standing for Christ's standards ... avoided opportunities to speak of the Lord ...?

Why the contradiction? Paul puts his finger on the answer; in practice not to be ashamed of Jesus means to **share in suffering** -

Read v 8 - 12.

Shame or suffering? Many Christians 'do a deal' and try to avoid both shame and suffering by purging their 'testimony' of everything unattractive or offensive. They merge into the world as if there were no difference between Christ's kingdom and Satan's kingdom. Such a testimony is a denial of Christ; they have successfully avoided the suffering but multiplied the shame.

There can be no 'deals'; the testimony of Christ's gospel is simply offensive. It is the testimony of ...

- **salvation.** That implies we need rescuing from our sins.
- **holy calling.** That implies God's initiative, calling us to a radically changed lifestyle.
- **grace not works.** That declares our powerlessness to please God, and His free undeserved gift of salvation.
- **eternal purpose.** That means God did the choosing before we ever appeared on the scene.
- **Jesus Christ.** That means death for us can only be abolished through His death on the cross.

Follow these themes through in v 9, 10. All highly offensive, all aimed at bringing man to his knees and exalting God, all guaranteed to meet resistance and opposition, all leading to **suffering.**

Shame or suffering? For Paul there was no hesitation - *read v 11, 12 again.*

For one thing it was **God** who had appointed him to teach this gospel; who was he to opt out when the going gets tough! But then again he had no desire to opt out. Even when chained and facing execution Paul could lift his head and shout out v 12.

Why? Because he knew **WHO** he was suffering for, he knew **Christ** Himself. And he knew that in urging Timothy to share in sufferings he was urging him into the fellowship of Christ's own sufferings - *read Philippians 3 v 10.*

Shame or suffering? Will you be ready now to bear clear, uncompromising testimony to the gospel that Paul and Timothy knew? Will you be ready to stop dodging the pain and face it as inevitable?

The answer partly depends on the value you put on knowing **WHO** you have believed.

Read 1 Peter 4 v 12 - 19.

Hold fast! 2 Timothy 1 v 13 - 18

What do we need - a faith that moves forwards or a faith that holds on?

The answer must be *both together!* We must avoid over-reacting against the head-in-the-sand mentality that cares nothing for progress so long as it manages to cling grimly to the old ways. We too must cling for all we are worth to the old truths if ever we are to make true progress;

Read v 13, 14.

Hold fast ... | The truths of God's Word are never isolated - they link together in a glorious design. As soon as we start picking and choosing which parts we will take notice of, the whole lot crumbles into ruins. Never give an inch on the wonderful truths that saved you - but what can you learn from the **spirit** in which we are exhorted to hold fast? | *... in faith and love*

Keep ... | Isn't it an amazing thing that God's weak, failing people are entrusted with a 'good thing' of such infinite value as the gospel? How can we be faithful when our understanding is so poor, our judgement so fallible, our wills so changeable, the pressures so powerful? But God has not given us an impossible task; He has given us the means as well as the task. Do you depend sufficiently on the Holy Spirit as you struggle to be faithful to the gospel? | *... by the Holy Spirit*

God has also given us another tremendous help in holding on to the truth. Real life examples! Just as Timothy could look to Paul's solid teaching, so many of us know older believers whose faith is firmly anchored on God's Word. Being loyal to the truth usually means being loyal to them. Sadly Paul's bitter experience is all too common today ...

Read v 15 - 18.
- **many turned away - v 15.** We do not know in what way these Asian believers had failed Paul (but compare with 4 v 10 - 16). Rather than speculating perhaps it would be more fruitful to think how you might have been unfaithful to other believers - and therefore unfaithful to the gospel.
- **Onesiphorus stood with Paul - v 16 - 18.** Whatever the cost, Onesiphorus had spared no pains in finding Paul, in prison at Rome, and providing for all his needs. And there does seem to have been a cost, for Paul prays for God's **mercy** to look after Onesiphorus and his family.
  often refreshed me ... not ashamed of my chain (imprisonment) ... very diligently ... how many ways he ministered to me.
  How many people could describe you in such glowing terms? Is your faithfulness to other believers a measure of your faithfulness to the gospel?
  Hold fast to God's words! Hold fast to God's people!

Read Hebrews 6 v 10; Matthew 25 v 34 - 40.

Be strong!   *2 Timothy 2 v 1 - 7*

Go for it, Timothy! You have heard all I have been saying in chapter 1 (refresh your minds), *now take courage in both hands and make the plunge ...* **Read v 1.**

Be strong ...	Isn't this a direct challenge to many of us whose Christian lives are so laid back, flabby, feeble, cowardly? We have been conditioned by a culture that tells us to avoid discomfort at all costs, let alone face up to pain and hardship.
in the grace ...	What an immense relief! Yes we ourselves must get stuck in, we must wade into battle, **but with Christ's resources.** Strong not in our own strength but in His - freely provided by His limitless grace! Now, however weak, however afraid, we are among those who can do all things through Christ who strengthens us. **Read Numbers 13 v 30 - 33.** Which group do you belong to?

And Timothy don't forget you are a leader. Be strong so you can spread the vision to others ... Read v 2.

commit these ...	Notice the chain: Paul - Timothy - faithful men - others. If the Word is to spread the chain must not stop with us. How concerned are you to share with others the truths that have delighted you?

Now Timothy stop to consider some illustrations. A Christian is to be a soldier, athlete and farmer all rolled into one...

Read v 3 - 7.

COMMITTED SOLDIER	A soldier has to be fed, clothed and housed like everyone else. The difference is that he is not distracted or tied down by everyday concerns. He never loses sight of being a soldier, ready to move, ready to fight at a moment's notice. Have you become 'entangled' by this world's affairs? So committed to your job ... your home ... even your family as to be no longer committed to the One who first called you to please Him?
DISCIPLINED ATHLETE	A runner cannot decide when to start, which lane to use, which direction to go, how far to run ... Unless he keeps to some very precise instructions he has no hope of winning. What kind of 'rules' could Paul have in mind for Timothy? (e.g. keeping to the 'lane' of God's Word). ***Compare with 1 Corinthians 9 v 24 - 27.***
HARDWORKING FARMER	Farmers simply **are** hard-working. They have to be if they want any crops to share in. Perhaps that is the clue to why many Christians are so lethargic. Is it because they have little desire, little expectation, little joy for souls saved? But what an encouragement as well as a challenge! Let us not grow weary while doing good, for in due season **we shall reap** if we do not lose heart (Galatians 6 v 9).

Like Paul, I have just dropped some hints to chew over. Take his advice in v 7.

Endure!   *2 Timothy 2 v 8 - 13*

Commitment ... discipline ... hard work ... **endurance**. Endurance is the fourth quality Paul urges on Timothy. Hanging in there when the going gets tough, pressing on when the pressure is on, sticking it out to the bitter end - yes even to death itself.

Read v 8 - 13.

CHRIST'S EXAMPLE - v 8

'Consider Christ' is the remedy for battle-fatigue. Did He give up half-way? Did He run away from mockery, beatings, crucifixion? Did He flinch from bearing all the wrath of God Himself for hell-deserving sinners? And what is it we are scared of facing in comparison to all that?! Notice the repeated 'endurance' theme in *Hebrews 12 v 1 - 4.*

Yet here in 2 Timothy 2 v 8, Christ's suffering to death is no more than **implied**. Paul's emphasis is more on the resurrection. Paul is saying *'I'm standing for the gospel that saw Jesus raised, so it is worth persevering'.* Yes resurrection follows suffering for those who endure with Christ!

PAUL'S EXAMPLE - v 9, 10

Few people could talk about endurance like the apostle. You name it, he had been through it. And he had made it - almost - to the end (see 4 v 6 - 8). Here he was, in chains, suffering as a common criminal under the inhuman Nero, telling us *'it's all worth it for my gospel!'* Why was it worth it? Paul tells us just two of many reasons;
- *the word of God is not chained!* The spread of the gospel does not depend on the availability even of the apostle Paul, let alone on any of us! Our plans might be thwarted but God can cause His word to run freely wherever He desires.
- *for the sake of the elect.* Ultimately what does it matter if I suffer and even die? What is that compared with the salvation of the people God has chosen for eternal life? They must have the gospel preached to them for they must be saved! Have we learned to think so selflessly ...?

A FAITHFUL SAYING - v 11 - 13

The two examples of enduring are backed up by an ENCOURAGEMENT and a WARNING. The four 'if' statements split into two pairs; the first pair promising us the rewards of enduring, the second pair threatening the consequences of faithlessness.
- **death leads to life, enduring to reigning.** True Christians are no strangers to death. Already they have died to self, died to this world. They have taken up the cross and become united to the death of their Saviour. But their Saviour now lives, now reigns - united to Him they too must live and reign!
- **denial leads to denial, faithlessness to faithfulness.** The last statement catches us by surprise, but there can be no alternative. God must remain faithful to His warnings as well as to His promises. It is an empty hope to imagine God will smile benignly on us in the end if we have deserted the faith. He will not, He cannot. *Matthew 10 v 32, 33.*

'Be faithful until death, and I will give you the crown of life' (Revelation 2 v 10)

Obstacle race   *2 Timothy 2 v 14 - 19*

You may not be like Timothy. You may be full of zeal and courage, itching to get stuck in to Christian service. Great ... but beware! The Christian life - and especially the Christian ministry - is more like an obstacle race than a straight run. Before we know it we will be flat on our faces unless we have a fifth quality - **discernment**. We need to know what to **avoid** as well as what to **go for**.

Read v 14 - 19.

- **AVOID SIDE-TRACKS (v 14).** Rather than getting hopelessly tangled up under the scrambling nets of irrelevant disputes, Timothy must urge his fellow teachers (v 2) to **avoid** them. For Timothy it was arguments over meanings of words etc (See 1 Timothy 1 v 3, 4; 6 v 3, 4). What for us are the petty side-tracks which can 'ruin the hearers' by distracting them from what really matters?

- **AVOID GODLESS ERROR (v 16 - 18).** For some the empty chatter of irrelevant arguments had turned into straight heresy. This is far more serious for it is designed not merely to delay us, but to put us out of the race altogether. Rather than give publicity and credibility to such error by entering into debate, Paul's instruction is to distance ourselves, avoid it, reject it out of hand.

- **GO FOR ACCURATE BIBLE-TEACHING (v 15).** Notice the key requirements for a Bible teacher. Someone who has his eyes on God's approval not man's, who works hard at understanding and presenting God's truth rather than speaking any nice thoughts that happen to occur to him, and who is careful to handle the Word rightly, bringing out its true meaning in context rather than using it to fit what he wants to say. If you are involved in any area of teaching, examine yourself using these requirements.

Yes there are great dangers, yes there are obstacles to distract us and obstacles to destroy us, yes we must exercise much discernment. NEVERTHELESS ... don't be put off, don't let your zeal be sapped ...

Read v 19 again.

Behind the scenes there is a solid foundation that cannot be moved. Christians may seem to us so weak, so vulnerable, so ready to fall away - but God's purposes cannot be thwarted, God's people cannot be lost.

Why? **Because God knows His people.** *John 10 v 14, 15, 27 - 30* says it all.

Why? **Because God's people leave their sin.** That is inevitable if God truly knows them. Sin as a way of life is finished. *1 John 3 v 4 - 9.*

Security and purity are the two sides of the one seal. They cannot be separated. Trust God to keep you safe **and** run from sin; then you have no need to fear the obstacles.

Useful for the Master   *2 Timothy 2 v 20 - 26*

As the Master surveys the 'house' of professing Christians for a 'dish' or 'spoon' suitable for serving Him, are you keen to be chosen? What kind of utensil is described as honourable, fit for the King to use?

Read v 20, 21.

The Master will not look for a silver dish amongst the pots and pans! We are not to be closely connected with those who bring dishonour to the Lord. He will look among those who are already set apart, clean and ready for His use. We are to be pure and holy, prepared through study and meditation of God's word, alert and ready to go at His command.

Paul enlarges on some of the personal qualities sought for by the Master:

- *Useful for the Master means fleeing from lusts* (v 22). It means resisting the pressures to be controlled by your own desires. *'Do it if you want to'* must be replaced by a new slogan; *'Do it if God wants you to'.* That applies to all age-groups, but it is when we are young that the passion is greatest, the pressure is greatest, the opportunities are greatest. And notice, resisting is by **running away**, not by keeping to 'sensible limits'!
- *Useful for the Master means pursuing values that please God* (v 22). How interested are you in these four qualities? Pursuing them does not mean simply agreeing that they are desirable, or even important. It means setting your heart on them, fixing your sights on them, thinking and planning and praying over how you may get them for yourself! It means making them a priority over all the other things you pursue - your relationships, your fitness, your sport, your exams - because God makes them a priority.
- *Useful for the Master means avoiding useless arguments* (v 23) Think how useless they are at doing anyone good. Not one of the virtues of v 22 will be produced by petty divisions - only quarrels!
- *Useful for the Master means having a right attitude towards opponents* (v 24 - 26). We are not to treat them as allies, not to compromise the truth or make pacts with them. We are indeed to fight for the truth ... but how?

Gently! We want to win them not beat them! And that is not by going in with all guns blazing at the slightest sniff of error, but by gently, patiently opening out God's Word to them.

Humbly! Are we any better than those who have fallen into false teaching? Only by God's grace do we remain faithful! **Humility** and **correction** are a rare but necessary combination.

Prayerfully! That is the implication of v 25. A longing for the Lord to bring them to the truth, knowing that our arguments alone will never be enough to bring about repentance.

Read carefully *2 Corinthians 10 v 1 - 6.*

Are you longing to be an instrument in the Lord's hands, used for His honour? Then spend a while searching your life with today's verses. What areas need attention? How in practice can you bring about those necessary changes, by God's power?

Perilous times, perilous men   *2 Timothy 3 v 1 - 9*

I do not think Timothy was ever imagining it would be easy! Yet it is easier to cope with difficulties if we know they are all scheduled. We are not to be wrong-footed by the apathy, the hard-heartedness, the opposition - we are told there will be times like this during the 'last days' (meaning, in the Bible, the whole gospel era).

Read v 1 - 5.

Reflect carefully on each description. I was planning on highlighting a few of the ones most relevant to our society, but try doing it yourself! How many seem **particularly** accurate? They all fit so well that it could have been written yesterday; unquestionably we live in a 'perilous time'.

The beginning and end provide the key that unlocks the foul chest;

lovers of themselves. Inevitably that leads to jealousy and self-indulgence and hatred and lies and a whole host of evil - because each person must put himself before others, whatever it takes.

... rather than lovers of God. The order of priority is me ... everything else ... God. God, who should be loved with all our heart, mind and soul takes last place - or no place at all.

And yet perhaps the most sinister description of them all is in v 5. **Many of these are professing Christians.** They come to church, go through the motions, perhaps even put on a nice Christian face for Sundays - and cynically deny it all by their lives.

Paul's instruction to us comes as a surprise - even though it is a theme he keeps repeating;
Avoid these hypocrites!

He tells us why; it is because they are dangerous! *Read v 6 - 9.* A certain type of person always falls for them. They are taken in by the winning personality and by easy assurances about their sinful lifestyle. They always get caught by the latest religious fad, eagerly drinking it in ... yet never coming to know the only truth that can **save** them (v 7).

Now we are not to be trapped like that. Many Christians say we cannot judge others, yet the Bible is constantly warning us to be discerning! At our peril we ignore Paul's instruction - and Jesus' - *read Matthew 7 v 15 - 20.*

That is hard! Especially as Christian charity makes us very slow to suspect others of hypocrisy. But in the end it will become painfully obvious whose side people are really on - *v 8, 9.*

Just as the magicians who copied the first plague in Moses' time were exposed as having no power to match God's, so will these people be seen as the empty showmen that they are.

Perilous times ... perilous men. Are you steering a safe course round them?

Living godly - by God's Word *2 Timothy 3 v 10 - 17*

'What do you do with 2 Timothy 3 v 12?' asked a Yugoslav (in the days of Communist persecution). The British pastor had no answer. Yes, he had freedom from persecution; but was it at the cost of godliness? What do **you** do with 2 Timothy 3 v 12? Do you suffer - are you godly?

Paul's challenge to Timothy is probably more than we would dare! *Examine my life! You have seen the way I have lived, you have seen the consequences of 'living godly in Christ Jesus'. Will you live like this - and suffer like this?*

Read v 10 - 13.

If you are in any leadership position you probably are already under the scrutiny of others, like it or not! What would they find under the nine headings of v 10, 11? Leader or not, it would be a well spent 9 minutes, though uncomfortable, to give just a minute to each.

Is Paul trying to put Timothy off? Persecution inevitable - oh and by the way it is likely to get worse rather than better as evil men grow more evil (v 13)!

Far from discouraging Timothy Paul urges him to **continue**. He must live by what he has learnt from childhood, whatever the cost -

Read v 14 - 17.

There is only one way to continue in the faith - **to live by God's Word**.
- **Convinced of it (v 14, 16)**. Timothy was sure the scriptures were true because he had seen them at work in his teachers (Lois, Eunice and Paul). In what other ways can we be sure that all God's Word is indeed **God's** word, 'God-breathed' (v 16) and totally reliable?
- **Trusting in it (v 15)**. There can be no salvation without knowing the truth in God's Word! Faith in Jesus comes through trusting the Bible's testimony of Him.
- **Using it (v 16)**. There is no substitute; both for controlling our own lives and instructing others. God's Word is not just for our 'quiet times' or for Sunday worship; it is to permeate every area of our lives. God's Word is to **teach** us the great truths about God, ourselves, salvation; God's Word is to **convict** us when we do wrong and to **correct** us so that we do right; God's Word is to **train** us to holy, God-honouring living.
Cultivate the habit of turning Bible reading into action. Always ask what use it can be put to in your life.

There is no other way for the Christian to live - and no other way to be equipped to serve God.

Read v 17 again. Do you want to be useful? Then be equipped by a working knowledge of God's Word. Study it, know it through and through until you have Bible-biased brains! But know it in practice too; know how to use it, know how to apply it, know how to live by it. *Read Psalm 119 v 99 - 112.*

I charge you   *2 Timothy 4 v 1 - 8*

Paul has reasoned and instructed, challenged and urged Timothy throughout the letter to throw himself into the thick of the battle.
Now as his parting shot he brings out the big guns -

I CHARGE you ... *Read v 1 - 5.*

You can't get more forceful than that! It was like an oath Paul was binding Timothy to - taken in the sight of the One who will judge our lives. How could Timothy ever face his Lord if he opted out of this solemn charge!

- **Preach!** That always must head the list. Preaching the word with God-given authority must never give way to modern user-friendly techniques.
- **Be ready!** A preacher does not feel like preaching? Too bad, he must go, relying on the Lord who commissioned him.
- **Convict!** Convince them of their sin and need. Never take away the cutting edge of the Word.
- **Rebuke!** Don't be afraid to identify specific weaknesses and sins of the congregation.
- **Exhort!** The people need not only to be taught but motivated. Persuasively urge their response.

Get on with it Timothy! Because your time is limited. While the people will listen make the most of every opportunity. Develop their taste for sound doctrine before they are lured by the tempting menus of half-truths (v 3, 4). What could be more relevant for today? What a challenge when people clamour for shorter, lighter sermons and more socials, to stir them to love the truth!

Get on with it Timothy! Because I can no longer. I am passing the baton on to you because my race is finished. Run like Linford Christie because the race must be won!

Read v 6 - 8.

What an amazing description of the end of Paul's life! Think about the expressions he chooses;

- **poured out.** We might say his life was ebbing away, but Paul sees even his last, weak days as a voluntary offering poured out to the Lord.
- **departure.** Paul had his destination firmly in view. Paul was not dying - he was going on a journey! He was waiting in the departure lounge longing to be there with Christ.
- **fought, finished, kept.** Paul was not leaving behind a half-finished assignment for others to pick up the pieces. There was no list of regrets at the end of a squandered, wasted life. He had fulfilled his commission, he had done what he could.

If we want to die like that we must live like Paul. Then, like him, we will have no fear of facing the righteous Judge, but will long for that Day when He will hand us the crown (v 8);
    'Well done, good and faithful servant. Enter into the joy of your Lord'

Read Paul's earlier debate about the end of his life; *Philippians 1 v 19 - 30.* What are the similarities and differences?

The Lord stood with me   2 Timothy 4 v 9 - 22

We might have thought Timothy had enough to be getting on with - but Paul needs him to fit in a trip to Rome before winter (v 9, 21)! Paul explains how he had been deserted for one reason or another; but surely it is not his own desire to see Timothy but the needs of the gospel that was behind Paul's request (v 11).

Read v 9 - 22 and take a look round with Paul at some of those he knew.

DEMAS
forsaken me
v 10

Demases rip pastors' hearts to bits. So promising, so useful at first - 'fellow labourers' in the gospel (Philemon 25). But then the deceitful attractions of the world show where their true affections lie. Gradually they slip away, sucked back into the world. Christian, examine yourself - *read 1 John 2 v 15 - 19.*

LUKE
with me
v 11

Lukes are gems. Always loyal, always there when you need them, to provide support, encouragement, practical help (though does v 16 suggest an exception?). They may not be gifted as teachers, but they are invaluable as encouragers. Could your Pastor say of you *'He/she is always with me'*?

MARK
useful to me
v 11

Marks are reasons for thanksgiving! You may remember that Mark had not always been useful - he had been a big disappointment in turning back home on mission. But he had come through! He had learnt from his failure and proved himself faithful. Perhaps you have shamefully failed the Lord - will you be a Mark?

ALEXANDER
did me harm
v 14, 15

Alexanders need guarding against. They are out to resist the truth and destroy the work. Yet we must also watch our own reaction to them. We are not to become bitter and vindictive over the damage they have caused, but leave it to the Lord to deal with them.

ALL
forsook me
v 16

Presumably referring to the trial at the end of Paul's **first** imprisonment; he had been bitterly disappointed by all those at Rome who could have been witnesses for him. There are times when even our most trusted friends will fail us - but what can we learn from Paul's response?

THE LORD
stood with me
v 17, 18

What a contrast to all the rest! He alone was faithful, He strengthened Paul, He delivered him from imprisonment for further missionary work. And, whatever anyone else may do to us, the Lord will **always** be there, rescuing us from all evil, preserving us for glory. There is only one response; *'To HIM be glory forever and ever!'*
Read Isaiah 41 v 8 - 13.

What a great encouragement to have fellow-workers in the gospel! What a joy to have people like Timothy to turn to for help! Yet, at the end of the day, *'vain is the help of man. Through God we shall do valiantly'* (Psalm 60 v 11, 12)

OUTLINE: 2 Timothy - Fight on!

> 'You therefore must endure hardship as a good soldier of Jesus Christ' (2 v 3)

☞ Sum up each section in a short sentence or phrase (ideas below).
☞ Look for key words in each section (usually repeated).

SECTION	SUMMARY	KEYWORDS
1 v 1- 7 v 8 - 12 v 13 - 18		
2 v 1 - 13 v 14 - 26		
3 v 1 - 9 v 10 - 17		
4 v 1 - 5 v 6 - 8 v 9 - 18 v 19 - 22		

God's man with God's Word ... preach while they will listen! ... finished and faithful ... stirring up Timothy's evident faith ... endure hardship ... perilous times and perilous men ... greetings and instructions ... but the Lord stood with me ... avoid useless teaching ... hold fast - some have turned away ... not ashamed of the gospel

FACT - FILE : Titus

> **TITUS**
>
> Good teaching for good living

THE SITUATION

- Titus is one of Paul's co-workers - though not mentioned in the book of Acts, so we know little about him. (But see the descriptions in 2 Corinthians 8 v 16, 17, 23.)
- At some time, possibly after Paul's first imprisonment at Rome, Titus had joined Paul in a mission to the island of Crete (See map on page 158). Paul left Titus at Crete to establish the new believers into local churches.
- Crete was no easy missionfield; Cretans had a notoriously bad reputation - and there were plenty of false teachers to bring out the worst in them.

THE LETTER

- Paul writes to reinforce the instructions he had left with Titus; especially to appoint leaders (elders) in every city, who were able to teach the word and oppose the false teachers.
- Paul emphasizes the need for **good works** to be the consequence of being saved by God's grace.
- Chapter 1 is concerned with **appointing suitable elders.** Chapters 2 and 3 focus on the **practical Christian living** Titus and these elders were to teach.

See fuller outline at the end of the section.

If at all possible ...

Find time to read the letter through in one sitting, with this background in mind.

Passing it on   *Titus 1 v 1 - 9*

Paul gives away his theme for this whole letter in the first verse:

TRUTH leading to GODLINESS

That is what they need to **'know'** or **'acknowledge'**; (meaning to know in practice not just in the head).
That is what will benefit the **'faith'** of these new Cretan believers.
That is what will keep their **'hope'** alive; their eager expectation of promised eternal life.

Read v 1 - 4.

Truth and godliness together. You cannot live right without knowing the truths of God's Word. You cannot truly know the truth if you are not living it out. Do you hold these two in the right balance? Does your Bible reading make a difference to your daily life?

If truth and godliness are so central, that is what must be taught! This is what had been committed to Paul (v 3), to Titus his 'son' and partner in the gospel (v 4); and now it was vital to commit it to faithful men throughout Crete. Titus could not do everything! In every city 'elders' or 'bishops' were needed who could be trusted to teach 'truth leading to godliness'. *See 2 Timothy 2 v 2.*

Read v 5 - 9.

What kind of men? Although Paul is obviously describing key characteristics for pastors / elders / bishops (the terms appear to be used interchangeably in the New Testament), isn't the question relevant for any one whose task it is to teach 'truth leading to godliness'? What kind of person? ... for Sunday School teachers, for Youth workers, for mission work. We must stop thinking 'who is available?' or 'who has volunteered?' and start using the searching tests of sections like this.

- ❏ *Blameless men* (v 6, 7). That seems to be like a heading for the lists that follow. Would anyone be able to point a finger, to see an inconsistency in his life?
- ❏ *Faithful men* (v 6). Faithful to his wife, faithful in bringing up his children. If he cannot control his household, he cannot be entrusted with leading the church.
- ❏ *Self-controlled men* (v 7). Not controlled by self-centred passions, but rather ...
- ❏ *Good-loving men* (v 8). They love to help others, love justice and holiness. For them 'self-controlled' means 'Spirit-controlled'.
- ❏ *Able to teach* (v 9). Stunningly obvious yet not always seen as important! Leaders who cannot teach are a contradiction; leading to Christ and leading to godliness means teaching truth!

Find similar tests in *1 Timothy 3 v 1 - 7.* Why similar? Why different in some details?

What kind of man? Who is to pass on the message of truth leading to godliness? In short, **godly** men who can teach the **truth**. Men who have grasped hold of truth-and-godliness in both hands. These are the kind of leaders we desperately need today. Pray for it!

Silence the false teachers!   *Titus 1 v 10 - 16*

What kind of men? Who were to be entrusted with spreading **truth** and **godliness**? Paul gives one further quality needed in good supply;
- *men who could contend for the truth - read v 9 - 16.*

They must face up to the opposition! In Crete there were 'many' (v 10) who refused to submit to God's truth, and they needed some pretty strong handling. The elders' job would be to ...
- **exhort;** (both the rebels and the waverers) to live by the Word of God (v 9).
- **convict;** to expose the sin of rebelling against God's authority (v 9).
- **silence;** to stop them spreading their cancerous teaching (v 10).

And it was not only the false teachers that needed strong handling! Cretans apparently had some dominant character traits that must be dealt with. **Sharp rebuke** was called for to rid them of tendencies which would wreck their faith and the church *(v 12, 13).*

> *'But everyone does it nowadays'* is no excuse for allowing lax standards in Christ's church. The right response is not to pedal softly but to target areas of weakness with special determination.

But, though the Cretans had a natural tendency to side with the false teachers, it is these rebellious men themselves who are the main problem to deal with. Look again at their characteristics in *v 10, 11, 14 - 16.*

The error itself is apparently to do with ceremonial purity. It is the familiar situation of Jews attempting to force Old Testament ceremonies onto Gentile believers - along with a whole batch of their own man-made Jewish traditions. But Paul will have none of it; the 'pure' are those who have been washed in the blood of Christ; they need no other, ceremonial purity! (v 14, 15)

But just as **truth leads** to **godliness**, so **error** leads to **ungodliness**. The stark, uncompromising descriptions Paul gives are startling. Pick them out from v 11, 15, 16.

Paul in no way gives the impression that these people are mostly good with one or two unfortunate defects! So far as he is concerned they are incapable of any good work (v 16); they are altogether enemies of the cross of Christ. *Read Philippians 3 v 1 - 3, 18, 19.*

> We must never assume that those who teach false doctrine are 'good at heart'. If, like these controversialists, they are teaching the 'commandments of men' instead of the Word of God, then it is likely that their lives are as bad as their teaching. *Read Jude v 3, 4, 16 - 19.*

Working alongside those with different views about the fundamentals of our faith is not 'Christian charity' - it is unchristian cowardice. Like Paul, like Titus, like the elders he was to appoint, leaders today must expose, discredit and silence those whose lives and teaching are *'abominable, disobedient, and disqualified for every good work'.*

It is a highly unfashionable task; highly unpopular, highly painful - but we duck out of it at the peril of the true church of Jesus Christ ...

Sound living   *Titus 2 v 1 - 10*

'But as for you ...' (v 1). The teaching of Titus (and the elders whom he would appoint) was to stand in stark contrast to that of those dangerous teachers just described. And the 'sound doctrine' was to include some very down-to-earth instructions for sound living.

Read v 1 - 10.

It is important not simply to scan through lists like these, but to spend a while chewing over each phrase; particularly in the sections that apply directly to you. What are the practical implications? How does it impact life at home, at work, at church? Does it touch areas of personal weakness?

There is only room here to sow seed-thoughts on just one phrase for each group;

- **Older men ... sound in faith** (v 2). Stop to do a spiritual health checkup. Your prayer-life, your Bible-reading, your relationships at home, church, work, college, your Christian service, your witness ... Younger Christians may show a certain imbalance, but is your walk with the Lord whole and healthy?
- **Older women ... teachers of good things** (v 3, 4). There is often social chit-chat; but how often are mature women busy teaching '**good** things'? To train the younger ones towards godly living is one of their key roles in the church!
- **Younger women ... homemakers** (v 5). Work outside of the home may be a necessity, but homemaking must be a priority for married women. We must not allow the world around us to twist our values; homemaking is one of the most vital, noble professions a woman can be called to.
- **Younger men ... sober-minded** (v 6). This is a theme throughout; the same word (in the original) is used in v 2, 5, 6 ('temperate', 'discreet', 'self-controlled'). It literally means 'saved in the mind'. We will never learn to live right until we learn to think right. *Romans 12 v 1, 2* combines the two perfectly.
- **Servants** (employees, students) **... all fidelity** (trustworthy) (v 9, 10). Not to need constant supervision, because when you have been assigned a task it will always be done - and done properly, on time, responsibly. Like a jewel is set to show up its beauty, so God's truth will sparkle brightly out of such a life. Joseph is a prime example: *Genesis 39 v 1 - 6, 20 - 23.*

Don't neglect this practical teaching - it is vital for the health of the church! But Paul has another message for Titus and all teachers.

Don't just say it, do it! Read v 7, 8 again.

- How were they to learn how to **live**? By watching Titus fill his life with good works!

- How were they to learn how to **approach God's Word?** By seeing the uncompromising, reverent, serious attitude of Titus. As he paid careful attention to what God has spoken, so they would know to mould their lives around the Word rather than the other way round.

- How were they to learn **how to speak**? By noticing Titus' healthy conversation. 'Spiritual' teaching must not be denied by empty, worldly chatter - so that even our opponents have to admit that our faith works.

Do you have examples like this? Then **follow** them ...

Teaching grace   *Titus 2 v 11 - 15*

'God's free grace in forgiving means I can be careless in living' may be the thinking of some - but not anyone who has really been touched by God's amazing free gift of salvation. Far from making believers careless, grace has some very different lessons to teach us -

Read v 11 - 15.

GRACE TEACHES US GODLINESS (v 12)

Isn't that the most wonderful way to learn how to live rightly? Moved not by the threat of punishment, nor even by the carrot of reward, but by amazed gratitude at the sheer love of the Saviour for me, even me. Why, if Jesus so willingly gave His life to bear the full punishment for my sins, how can I willingly sin another sin? If He shed His precious blood to bring me, His enemy, to peace with God, how can I ever grieve and alienate Him again?

'Love so amazing, so divine
Demands my soul, my life, my all'

GRACE TEACHES US TO LOOK FORWARD (v 13)

Why do believers hope confidently for heaven? Because they have already tasted God's grace! The God who has freely forgiven them will freely take them to glory! The Saviour who has appeared once to freely die for their sins will appear again to freely bring them to Himself. *Romans 8 v 32* assures us that our confidence is not misplaced!

Have you learnt this lesson, though? Are you eagerly straining towards heaven, fixing your sights on knowing that 'blessed hope' as a glorious reality? Do you long to see Jesus appearing in all His majestic glory as God-Saviour?

GRACE TEACHES US TO VALUE REDEMPTION (v 14)

Free grace is costly grace. That is why it is so amazing! What was purchased at infinite price is given freely to undeserving wretches! Value redemption by responding in love ...

- **He gave Himself for us.** What a gift to us who are Christians! What a sacrifice! And do we hold back ourselves?
- **He purchased us.** We belong to Him! We are no longer our own.
- **From all wickedness.** That was His great purpose - do we now cling to the sin He rescued us from?!
- **His own special people.** He is jealously possessive of us - yet are we keen to share our allegiance with the world ...?

Read v 15 again.

Titus, teach these things! And do not be content with teaching them - exhort the people until they respond in loving obedience to God's amazing grace. And if still they are unmoved, rebuke them for their dull hearts! One thing is vital - those saved by God's grace must live by God's grace, *'zealous of good works'* (v 14c). Does that describe you?

Read Romans 6 v 1, 2, 14 - 18.

Have you noticed Paul's approach? Practical instructions (2 v 1 - 10) reinforced by powerful motivation (2 v 11 - 14). He uses the same formula in chapter 3, moving away from behaviour in the church to behaviour in society; *read v 1 - 7.*

GOOD WORKS TO ALL MEN - v 1, 2

How often do we hear it; respected deacon in the church, but shady business deals at work; zealous for evangelism in the town, but lazy and awkward in the factory. Such Jekyll-and-Hyde Christianity is foreign to Paul.

- **Good citizens.** Here is an opportunity to be different! While others complain endlessly and fiddle instinctively, Christians can gladly pay their taxes and knuckle under legislation, grateful for the structure and order that God has given us. *Read 1 Peter 2 v 13 - 17.*
- **Good neighbours.** Notice how uncomfortably comprehensive verse 2 is! Christian virtues shine brightest where they are most needed! How Christlike to have no evil to speak against the most unpleasant person, to be peacemaking and humble towards the most arrogant individual ...

Listen to Jesus; *Matthew 5 v 16.*

GOOD REASONS FOR ALL BELIEVERS - v 3 - 7

Is it hard to submit to harsh, ungodly government? Is it impossible to remain gentle and caring towards that bitter, scheming, foul-mouthed colleague? How good then to review the way God's love shone down on us in all our foulness ...

- **We were obnoxious** (v 3). Perhaps others saw us as reasonably pleasant, but God knew every atom of the filth, the self-centredness, the rebellion, that saturated us. Are we not ashamed of the remaining malice, hate and hatefulness that spoils the way we treat others?
- **We were loved** (v 4, 5). When we were most unlovable, God's love and kindness appeared to save us! When we were lost in the quagmire of our own sin, deserving nothing but God's rejection and anger, His mercy and grace was freely shown to us. So will we reach out in love to others in their sin and need? Or will we wait first for them to deserve our help and sympathy?
- **We were renewed** (v 5, 6). Is it so impossible to be Christlike towards others? Do we despair of ever living as we should? Yes, if it were not for what God has done for us! But He has washed us from our sins, He has given us the new birth ('regeneration'), He has made us a new creation in Christ, He has freely lavished on us His own Holy Spirit! Never complain of being powerless - live by the power of the Holy Spirit within you.
- **We were made heirs** (v 7). Eternal life beckons us upwards. More than that, eternal life has begun within us! Already we are heirs if we are in Christ; we have begun the life of sons and daughters of God who will live and reign as co-heirs with Christ for ever! This is true, but do our friends and neighbours and workmates see it? Do they recognise that we are not one of them, but sons and heirs of God?

Now go back to v 1, 2. Have you been stirred to respond in amazed gratitude at God's love even for you?

Final instructions *Titus 3 v 8 - 15*

Paul has made his theme pretty clear; but he wants to make sure it becomes the theme of Titus and all the elders appointed in Crete. *Read v 8 - 11.*

Keep stressing these things! (v 8)

Some preachers seem to have a hobby horse which somehow manages to creep into most of their sermons! Paul gives Titus his hobby horse - it is to be **doctrine leading to godliness!** The teaching was not to be theoretical and dry as dust, but always practical and applied. The glorious truths of redemption (such as the 'faithful saying' of v 4 - 7) are taught not only to warm our hearts but to stir us to good works.

Avoid foolish disputes! (v 9)

Contrast the end of v 8 with the end of v 9. That gives us the guidelines for what today is to be avoided. If something is not doing us good then leave it alone! If it leads to arguments and conflict over what the Bible does not emphasise, then concentrate on truths spurring you to godliness!

Reject divisive false teachers! (v 10, 11)

Does that sound too harsh, too uncompromising?
>No, because the great aim is to **win** not to reject; it is only after repeated rejection of loving warnings that they themselves must sadly be rejected.
>No, because it is out of tender concern for God's people; they must not be harmed by divisive teaching.
>No, because the glory of God is in view; His truth must be jealously guarded.

Paul's letters to Timothy are full of similar instructions; e.g. *read 1 Timothy 6 v 3 - 6; 2 Timothy 2 v 14 - 26.*

Paul was a very down-to-earth man. He is not so preoccupied with his burden for Crete that he has no time for practical arrangements. *Read v 12 - 15.*

Come to me at Nicopolis! (v 12)

Note the balance in this verse; the work at Crete was not to be dependent on Titus being there - but neither was it to be left unsupervised. **Sharing responsiblity responsibly** is vital for Christian leadership; does that apply to your own situation?

Help Zenas and Apollos on their way! (v 13, 14)

Presumably these men were delivering the letter; perhaps on a missionary tour. Titus was not to be so wrapped up in his own work so as to neglect these other workers. And v 24 probably implies that he was to involve others in the church to help and encourage them. This is just the point of the whole letter - Christians have got to learn to give themselves to good works. Here is a practical example of how they can begin!

Greetings! (v 15)

For Paul this was no mere formality. He had a big heart that loved to send greetings to his fellow believers in Christ. How we need our love to be stirred for believers in other churches so that it warms our hearts to think of them!

OUTLINE: Titus - good teaching for good living

> '...*these things I want you to affirm constantly, that those who have believed in God should be careful to maintain good works.*' (3 v 8)

- Sum up each section in a short sentence or phrase (ideas below).
- Look for key words in each section (usually repeated).

SECTION	SUMMARY	KEYWORDS
1 v 1 - 4 v 5 - 9 v 10 - 16		
2 v 1 - 10 v 11 - 15		
3 v 1 - 7 v 8 - 11 v 12 - 15		

appoint elders to teach ... practical arrangements ... good reasons for good works ... the motives of grace ... silence false teachers ... sound living for all ages ... teach godliness, avoid useless disputes ... entrusted to apostle and son

FACT - FILE : *Philemon*

> **PHILEMON**
>
> Receiving a brother

THE SITUATION

- Philemon was a key member of the church at Colosse and renowned for is love to the saints.
- His slave, Onesimus, had escaped, met up with Paul in prison at Rome and been converted. Previously useless, he was now a valuable worker.

THE LETTER

- The author is Paul, writing from his house-prison in Rome.
- Written around AD 62, at the same time as his letter to the whole church at Colosse ('Colossians').
- Its purpose is to urge Philemon to receive Onesimus back as his slave - and Christian brother.
- The first seven verses commend Philemon's faith and love; the rest of the letter argues Paul's case.

    (Since the letter is so brief, and simple in purpose and structure, there is no outline at the end of the section.)

If at all possible ...

Find time to read the letter through in one sitting, with this background in mind.

Refreshing example   *Philemon v 1 - 7*

There is a world of difference between buttering people up to get what you want, and showing your genuine love and appreciation for them. We are quick to notice when others are exceptionally complimentary; our immediate guarded reaction is 'what do they want now?'

Paul's love for Philemon was not put on. He was in the habit of thanking God for fellow-believers - and the reports he had heard of Philemon genuinely thrilled him. Philemon's reaction would not be a cynical 'what does he want now?', but a warm 'How can I respond in love to him?'

Read v 1 - 7.

Philemon's example is a challenge to us. When our pastor or other believers think of us, are they flooded with joy and encouragement as in verse 7? We will look briefly at the characteristics of Philemon that so delighted Paul:

- **Philemon was a fellow-labourer** (v 1, 2)
  Paul was in love with the gospel - and with anyone who shared that love. He could only be in one place at a time, but to think of others working away in other towns and churches greatly encouraged Paul. Notice how fellow-labourer Philemon welcomed the church at Colosse into his home, v 2, and how Archippus (probably his son) also shared in the gospel work. (But compare with Colossians 4 v 17).
  Are you a fellow-labourer?

- **Philemon's love and faith were newsworthy** (v 5, 6).
  Probably **'love'** should be linked to 'all saints', and **'faith'** to 'the Lord Jesus' (as NIV, compare Colossians 1 v 4). The two belong together; if our faith really is strong in the Lord, then others will experience the strong love that goes along with it. A faith that does not produce love is no faith.
  And Philemon's love was not choosy. It was for **all** saints, however difficult they might be to love. And, although the exact meaning of verse 6 is debatable, its basic thrust is clearer - Paul is praying that the 'all' might include runaway slave Onesimus.
  How would others describe your love? Widespread? Obvious? Strong?

- **Philemon was refreshing** (v 7).
  Recently a lady who had been visiting a church for a while said afterwards; 'I learnt more from the people than from the preaching; I've never known anything like it'. She explained how refreshed and challenged she had been by the self-sacrificing love she had been shown ... Philemon was like that. Not only was he hospitable, but people went away with something they would not quickly forget. Their **hearts** had been done a power of good.

Philemon had already refreshed Paul, but Paul still asks for more - *verse 20.* Will you respond to that plea, and set out by God's grace to be like a breath of fresh air to fellow-believers? Read further refreshing examples in *Philippians 2 v 25 - 30; 2 Timothy 1 v 16 - 18.*

Tactful persuasion — *Philemon v 8 - 16*

Paul's main task is to persuade Philemon to receive his errring slave Onesimus. However useful Onesimus was to Paul, Paul knew he belonged to Philemon. And it was no half-hearted effort he makes; let's learn from his approach; *read v 8 - 16*.

Paul prefers the arguments of love to apostolic authority (v 8, 9). He could have demanded, but preferred to plead. He wanted to treat Philemon as a dear brother, rather than exercising authority over him.

If we are in a position of authority it can be so much easier to **instruct**. But if we value our brothers and sisters we will take the time to use loving persuasion...

Paul's arguments are passionate and persuasive. A loving approach does not mean a spineless, flabby one. Despite the fact that he stands to lose personally, Paul's appeal is crammed full of potent reason.

Let's not be afraid to use strong biblical arguments to persuade people. Merely dropping a gentle hint may be a cop-out rather than caring counsel.

Paul's arguments are full of tact. That does not mean, as so often, flattery and dishonesty. It means the arguments are designed with Philemon's feelings in mind - yet without losing any of their force.

How you say it is just as important as what you say. The purpose is to win the person, not just the argument - and that means putting ourselves in their shoes.

Notice those features as you follow the implied arguments with the verses:

- *Really I'm asking a small thing compared with the hardships I have endured.* (v 9)
- *I love him as a son; please do the best for him.* (v 10, 12)
- *He is not what he used to be; he has become as his name means, Profitable.* (v 11)
- *It's really a sacrifice to let him go; but it wouldn't have been right to hold on to him and presume on your generosity.* (v 13, 14)
- *God's hand was over-ruling his escape, bringing him to me that I might return him to you in a new relationship.* (v 15)
- *He is now a believer! To receive him back will be a double blessing; you will gain a faithful servant and a loved brother.* (v 16)

Learn from another example of tactful argument - Abigail in *1 Samuel 25 v 14 - 35*.

Three brothers   *Philemon v 17 - 25*

What should be the Christian's approach to social concerns? We might expect this letter to give some valuable pointers, but on first reading we are disappointed. We look in vain for condemnation of the cruelties and injustice of slavery. In fact Paul seems quite content with the status quo as he urges Philemon to receive Onesimus back - as a slave...

Yes, as a slave - but a slave with a difference! How else is Philemon to receive Onesimus?

Read v 16, 17.

- *Receive him as a loved brother!* They were now one in Christ. The master-slave relationship still held, but it must not interfere with a new brother-brother relationship. And this certainly amounts to a new concept in slavery! *See Galatians 3 v 28, 29.* Compare with *Leviticus 25 v 39 - 43.*
- *Receive him as myself!* If you want a yardstick as to how far to go in welcoming Onesimus, it's this - treat him as you would treat me! Treat him as most important guest or closest friend! Yes, treat him as an apostle of Jesus Christ!

Certainly this letter announces no grand apostolic plan to abolish slavery. In fact it works within the framework of a corrupt system. Yet if Philemon puts Paul's guidelines into action, don't you think that word would quickly get around as to what the gospel does for slaves?

We can think on too grand a scale. If we are concerned about social injustice (as indeed we should be) let's start at home. Start by ripping down those social, racial, economic barriers between brothers. Start by treating one another as equals, or rather as Christ's special people. See what that gospel does for social issues!

Will Philemon really be able to forget the tensions and bad experiences of the past, and love Onesimus like this? Paul uses another argument designed for maximum impact!

Do it for me! Read v 17 - 25.

Paul knew how indebted Philemon felt towards Paul. He would surely do anything for the one to whom he owed his very spiritual life; who was the means God had used to bring him to faith (v 19). Though Paul is genuinely willing to pay back anything that Onesimus had stolen, the way he phrases his offer is designed to show Philemon that he understands how inappropiate Philemon would feel that to be (v 18, 19). Yes, surely Philemon would jump at this opportunity to repay Paul with 'joy' and to 'refresh his heart' (v 20). When Paul comes to visit, there will be no embarrassment (v 22); instead the three brothers will rejoice together in the goodness of God.

Do it for me!
What you ought to do may be hard, but will you do it for the sake of refreshing some dear friend, and the Lord Himself ...?

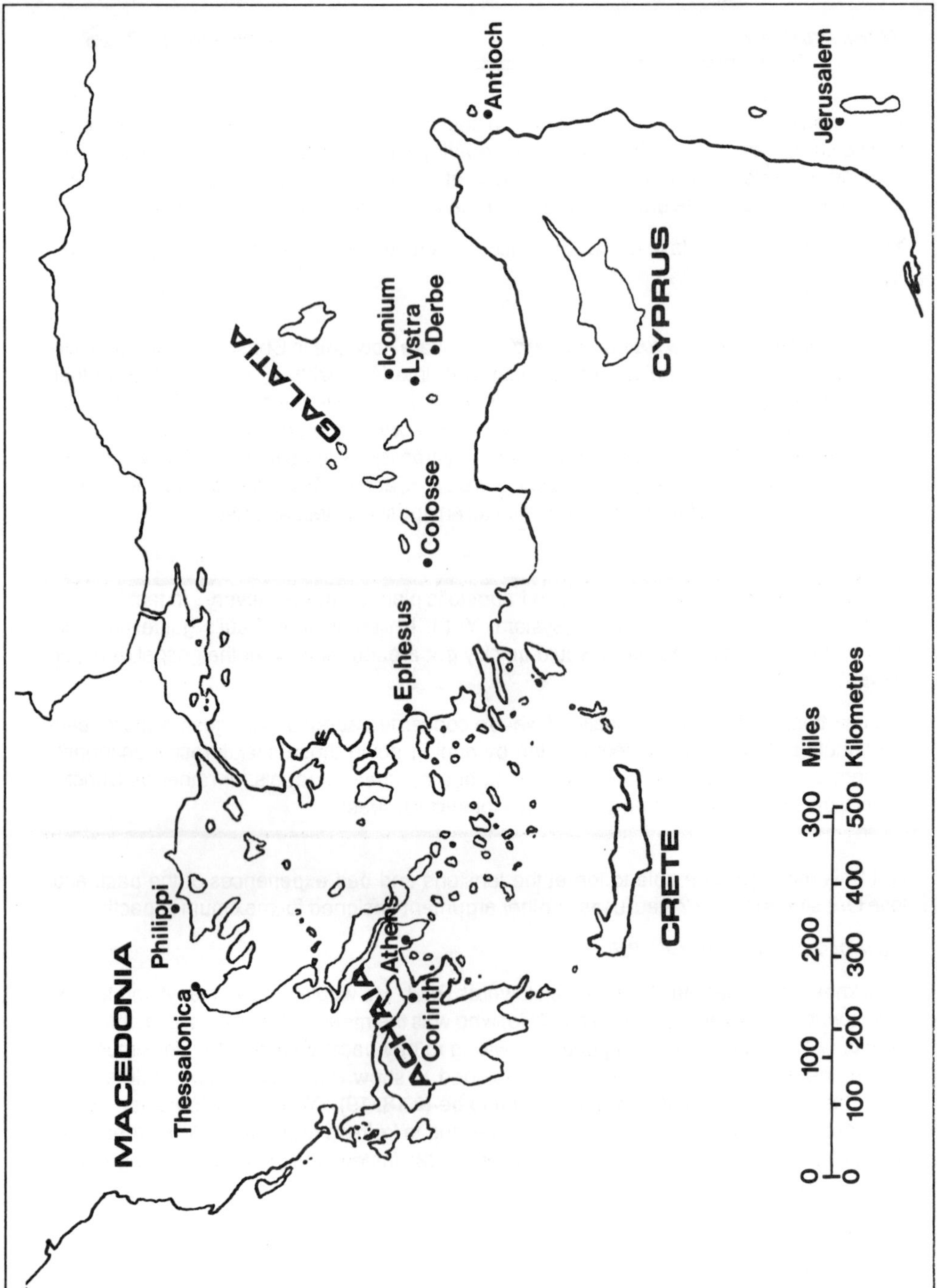
MACEDONIA
Thessalonica
Philippi
ACHAIA
Athens
Corinth
CRETE
Ephesus
Colosse
GALATIA
Iconium
Lystra
Derbe
CYPRUS
Antioch
Jerusalem
0 100 200 300 Miles
0 100 200 300 400 500 Kilometres

encourage ...
BIBLE READING
in your family

DISCOVER (11 - 15)
DAILY BIBLE NOTES

(adult)   ## EXPLORE
DAILY BIBLE NOTES

➡ Challenging ... attractive ... no gimmicks
➡ Accuracy a key aim

Send for sample issues!
(Please enclose £1.00 towards cost, for each sample requested.)

DISCOVER
Publications, Arisaig, Crowborough Hill, Crowborough, E.Sussex, TN6 2EA